ULSTER
Walk guide

Richard Rogers

Gill and Macmillan

Published in Ireland by
Gill and Macmillan Ltd
Goldenbridge
Dublin 8
with associated companies in
Auckland, Budapest, Gaborone, Harare, Hong Kong,
Kampala, Kuala Lumpur, Lagos, London, Madras,
Manzini, Melbourne, Mexico City, Nairobi,
New York, Singapore, Sydney, Tokyo, Windhoek
© Richard Rogers 1980, 1991
First published in 1980 under the title
IRISH WALK GUIDES/4: NORTH EAST
Second edition published 1991
Reprinted 1992
0 7171 1912 2
Print origination by
Joe Healy Typesetting, Dublin
Printed by
The Guernsey Press Co. Ltd, Guernsey

Based upon the Ordnance Survey map
with the sanction of the
Controller of HM Stationery Office,
Crown Copyright reserved (Permit No. 400)

A catalogue record for this book is
available from the British Library.

For Kitty

CONTENTS

KEY TO SYMBOLS USED IN MAPS

Start of Walk ●

Finish of Walk ■

Deciduous Plantation

Coniferous Plantation

Access roads/tracks × × × ×

Dick Rogers has since boyhood enjoyed walking in the hills and coastlands of his native Ulster. An early youth hosteller, he became interested in conservation and has been associated with the work of the National Trust in Northern Ireland since its inception. As Secretary for eight years of the Ulster Countryside Committee and of the Nature Reserves Committee he was able to work for the protection of the areas through which most of the walks here described are made.

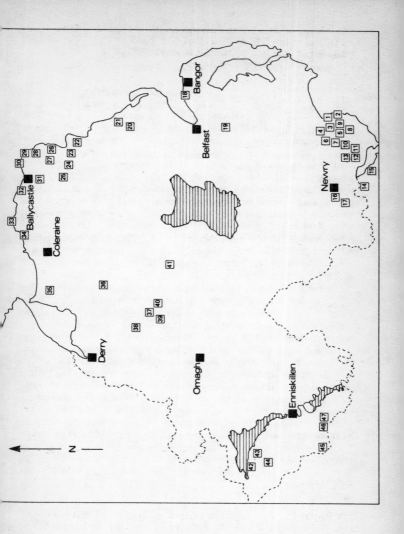

PREFACE

I was delighted when Fergal Tobin told me that, although *North East* had gone out of print, Gill and Macmillan proposed to publish the text again under a new title.

The Walks described here are hill walks. I make an exception of the Antrim Coast, for the Antrim plateau falls into the sea and you can have the excitement provided by difficult terrain, e.g. at Fair Head, associated with the compulsive attraction of an incomparable landscape. There are two other exceptions: the Lagan Towpath and the Holywood to Bangor Coastal Path.

The walks are all in Northern Ireland, except two in North Louth which are included because of the proximity of the Carlingford Mountains to those of South Down and South Armagh. We in Ulster are proud of our natural heritage, and even in a short walking holiday the visitor may detect that love of country which has enabled some areas to be given broad protection as Areas of Outstanding Natural Beauty, Areas of Special Scientific Interest or to be carefully conserved as National Nature Reserves. He will also meet those characteristics of independence and forthrightness which are typical of the Ulsterman, as well as kindliness and humour.

Hill walkers respect the countryside and its people; they don't gather wild flowers (especially rare species), don't disturb nesting birds, leave no litter, close gates, walk at the side of fields with crops, and are careful to avoid damaging stone walls and fences. I have never been forbidden to go on mountain land, but changes in ownership and in farming methods may arise, bringing marginal land into cultivation, and in one or two places in the book I have indicated that it would be well to ask the landowner's permission to cross his land. The people of the hills are always friendly and helpful and you can best repay them by talking to them, asking their advice about the weather or the way, and treating their property with respect.

In estimating the time for each walk I have followed the rule: one hour for each three miles, and one hour for each 1,500 feet of ascent. The times taken for the walks vary from two hours to one of nine hours. This last, which I have called 'Nine Summits', covers 19½ miles in the northern range of the Sperrins. The average time overall in the book is about five hours. You should allow extra time for viewing, eating, resting and so on.

I have tried to provide for youth hostellers by basing the walks on hostels where they are available. I have also catered for the car-assisted walker by describing a number of walks starting and ending in the hills at a point identified by a grid-reference as well as by description.

The Northern Ireland Ordnance Survey issued some years ago a Third series of maps, scale 1" to the mile. Sheet 9 covers the Mournes and the Carlingford Mountains; Sheet 8, Armagh; Sheets 1 and 3, Antrim and Binevenagh; Sheets 2 and 5, Benbradagh and the Sperrins; Sheets

4 and 7, Fermanagh. These maps are now difficult to obtain, but the Ordnance Survey have issued a new Discoverer series, scale 1:50,000, about 1¼ inches to one mile. The route maps in this book are based on the one-inch map, but the text and the route map for each walk can be followed whether you use the one-inch map or the more detailed and modern Discoverer map.

The bibliography had to be brief. We are all particularly indebted to two Ulstermen, Robert Lloyd Praeger, who knew every townland in Ulster, and E. Estyn Evans, who knew every stone, custom and tradition. The visitor may be surprised to find a reference to a guide issued in 1924 by a now extinct railway company. The reason is that Praeger wrote a very comprehensive guide for the railway company in 1900 which is now rare, but the 1924 guide still contains much that was written by him.

I should like to thank again those who helped me in the publication of 1980. In particular Ivor McDonald for checking the fauna section of the Introduction and Joe Furphy for checking and revising the flora section and for his advice on birds and on rare plant species. Again my thanks are due to Alan Warner and Wilfrid Capper; John Phillips, Geoffrey Coates, Bill Wright and Charlie Farmer of (or retired from) the Forestry Division, Department of Agriculture; William Robb, James Marsh and the late George Doyle.

My appreciation also to Fergal Tobin for his patience and helpfulness and to Henry Sharpe for drawing the route maps.

My final thanks go to my late wife Kitty for the initial drafting of the maps, for her encouragement and indulgence, and above all for lightening many a mile.

Dick Rogers,
Castle Espie,
Comber, Co. Down.
May 1991

AUTHOR

Dick Rogers has since boyhood enjoyed walking in the hills and coastlands of his native Ulster. An early youth hosteller, he became interested in conservation and has been associated with the work of the National Trust in Northern Ireland since its inception. As secretary for eight years of the Ulster Countryside Committee and of the Nature Reserves Committee, he was able to work for the protection of the areas through which most of the walks here described are made. He was awarded the OBE in 1960. He was Associate Editor of the *AA Tourist Guide to Ireland* (1976) and, as co-author of *Castle, Coast and Cottage* (The Blackstaff Press, 1986), he wrote the history of the National Trust in Northern Ireland.

INTRODUCTION

Climate and Weather

The climate of the north east of Ireland, like that of the whole island, is shaped by two factors, the westerly atmospheric circulation, and the proximity of the Atlantic Ocean. These factors interact to give us westerly winds, mild damp weather and a small temperature range throughout the year.

Although the weather is very variable, certain climatic features seem to occur with some regularity. During December and January, there is a well-established low-pressure system over the Atlantic, producing depressions which move rapidly eastwards bringing strong winds and abundant frontal rain. By late January the cold anti-cyclonic weather centered over Europe may be extending westwards into Ireland giving dry, cold spells, eminently suitable for hill walking. From February to June the cold European anti-cyclones, reinforced sometimes by a southward extension of the Greenland anti-cyclone, tend to produce the driest period of the year. Towards late June or early July the pressure rises over the ocean and falls over the continent, initiating a westerly, damp airflow over Ireland. Cloud cover, humidity and rainfall increase and thunder becomes more prevalent, especially during the warmer periods of August. Cold northerly air may bring active depressions in late August and September, but these can be interrupted by spells of anti-cyclonic weather. In October and November rain-bearing westerlies predominate, though an incursion of anti-cyclonic conditions can bring blue skies and pleasant walking conditions. The prevailing winds are south-westerly and westerly, but winds from the north and east may occur with anti-cyclonic conditions. The winds are lightest from June to September, and strongest from November to March.

May tends to be the sunniest month with around six hours a day, falling away through June to four and a half hours a day in July.

As noted above, the spring is the driest part of the year, and, though the ground underfoot is still very wet from the autumn and winter rains, March, April and May are perhaps the best months for walking.

In general rainfall decreases as one moves east, though this tendency is hardly noticeable in the mountain areas. Snow is uncommon in our maritime climate, rarely persisting for long, even at high level, though in some winters it may lie for several weeks in high north-facing coombes and gullies.

The sea-level rainfall in the north-east falls from some 1,100 mm. a year in western parts to 900 mm. in the east. The mountain areas, however, all act as cloud catchers, and rainfall in the Mournes, Sperrins and Antrim hills exceeds 1,600 mm. annually. In terms of wet days the Mournes are slightly drier, averaging some 180 wet days annually as compared with over 200 wet days in the other hill areas (a wet day being defined as one on which more than 1 mm. of rain falls). All this means that you should carry raingear whenever you go walking, but the main characteristic of Irish weather is its variability, and most of these 200 wet days will have fine spells, when you will be very glad that you persevered with your walk in spite of the showers.

Access and Accommodation

There are car ferry sailings into Belfast from Liverpool; into Larne from Stranraer; into Larne from Cairnryan; and into Belfast from Douglas, Isle of Man. There is also a direct car ferry service between Ireland and the continent, using the ports of Le Havre (France) and Rosslare in south-east Ireland.

There are air services to Aldergrove, ten miles west of Belfast, from all parts of the British Isles. Trains run between Belfast, Londonderry, Coleraine, Larne and Bangor. There is an express train service between Belfast and Dublin. Ulsterbus has road services to all parts of Northern Ireland except some mountain areas. Northern Ireland is exceptionally well provided with roads. Traffic is light and in the walking country covered by this book visitors from abroad will find the roads very quiet except prehaps at weekends or in peak holiday periods.

The Youth Hostel Association of Northern Ireland provides simple accommodation in a chain of four hostels on the Antrim coast; a chain of four hostels in South Down; a chain of three hostels in the mountains of Londonderry and Tyrone; and a hostel in Belfast. Information from YHANI, 58 Bradbury Place, Belfast (Telephone 084–324733.) There is hotel, guest house, farm-house or country-house accommodation in most areas. Information from Tourist Information Centre, 59 North Street, Belfast BT11NB (Telephone 084–246609.)

A number of Mountaineering and Rambling Clubs, who welcome visitors on their outings, are based in our area. Addresses of Mountaineering Clubs may be obtained from the Federation of Mountaineering Clubs of Ireland, 3 Gortnamona Drive, Dublin 18, and of Ramblers Clubs from the Sports Council for Northern Ireland, House of Sport, Upper Malone Road, Belfast (Telephone 084–381222.)

There are four Mountaineering Club huts in the Mournes, which can be generally used by members of Mountaineering Clubs from abroad. Details from FMCI.

The Northern Ireland Mountain Centre is situated at Tollymore, north of the Mourne Mountains. It conducts instructional courses in walking and general mountaineering, and the staff will give local advice.

Geology

The southern part of Down and Armagh has the highest and most striking mountains in the region, in the Tertiary granite Mourne Mountains and the basic intrusive rocks of Slieve Gullion with its encircling ring-dyke. This igneous complex is completed by the intrusive acid and basic rocks of the Cooley peninsula in north Louth on the south side of Carlingford Lough, a typical fiord of great beauty.

The Tertiary lava plateau of Antrim and east Londonderry is gently folded down the middle from north to south to form the valley of the Lower Bann. To the west and east the plateau rises to heights of well over 1,000 ft and on all sides, except the south west, presents steep escarpments. Along the north and east Antrim coasts the basalts and underlying chalk (or limestone as we call it here) give headland after headland of dramatic quality and varied colour, in some places black

9

basalt and white limestone giving place to red sandstone. To the west the basalt scarp towers over the plain of north Londonderry; to the south in the Lagan Valley the basalt hills form a backdrop for the activity of half the population of Northern Ireland.

In south Londonderry and Tyrone the topography is related to the strong Caledonian trends of north-west Ireland. But east of the Foyle-Mourne-Strule basin the grain of the country is ill-defined and, whereas Donegal (included in another book in this series) has a highly dissected terrain with rugged pinnacles and ridges, south Londonderry and Tyrone have a gentle outline with relics of a high plateau forming the long, lazy, rounded Sperrin Mountains.

To the west is the great Erne basin on carboniferous limestone. Heathery hills of metamorphic rocks fringe Lower Lough Erne in the north-west, and of Old Red Sandstone in the north-east; while south-west of Lower Lough Erne, between it and Lough Macnean, Yoredale sandstones overlying the limestone form a high moorland, with heathery hills which stretch south, culminating in Cuilcagh (2,188 ft) on the borders of Fermanagh and Cavan. Fringing the sandstone hills are others of limestone.

Flora and Fauna

Flora   I shall describe the flora of the areas in which the walks are grouped, commencing with the Mourne Mountains. Being a comparatively young group of mountains with poor, acid soil and steep slopes, the Mournes do not have a rich flora, but there is much of interest. You will find the small rosettes of the Starry Saxifrage *(Saxifraga stellaris)*; in a few rock crevices the yellow Roseroot *(Rhodiola rosea)*; in one or two of the gravelly lakes the pale lilac Water Lobelia *(Lobelia dortmanna)*. Much more widespread among the heathery boulders the abundant black berries of Bilberry *(Vaccinium myrtillus)* may be found in autumn, and on the summits the scarlet berries and evergreen leathery leaves of Cowberry *(V. vitis-idaea)*. The summits also have swards of *Rhacomitrium* and frequently also Dwarf Mountain Willow *(Salix herbacea)*; Juniper *(Juniperus communis)* occurs more sparingly. Much of the area is dominated by grassland, with Mat-grass *(Nardus stricta)* abundant; among the other grasses is the tall Wood Fescue *(Festuca sylvatica)*. There are many boggy stretches, with Bog Asphodel *(Narthecium ossifragum)*, and also Sundew *(Drosera rotundifolia)*, the species with a rosette of red leaves. Other damp sites yield sedges, including the Slender-leaved Sedge *(Carex lasiocarpa)*. There are various members of the genus *Hieracium* including, on Pigeon Rock and Eagle Mountain, *H. sagittatum,* and in Tollymore Forest Park, *H. senescens;* this last-named locality is rich in scarce species and also has a fine arboretum. The alien *Rhododendron ponticum* was originally introduced as undergrowth in a wood at Kinnahalla; the wood was cut down many years ago, but the rhododendron has spread over several acres of hillside, making a wonderful sight in May, and providing a valuable roosting site for birds in winter.

When you move to the Antrim glens and moors you will discover a rich and varied landscape. The great variety of rocks, frequently exposed in lofty cliffs, leads to alternations of black basalt, white limestone and red sandstone, contrasting with the green of the grassland and the brown and purple of the moorlands.

In the glens masses of Primroses *(Primula vulgaris)* are to be seen, with sheets of Wild Hyacinth or Bluebell *(Endymion non-scriptus)* and many of the richly coloured Early Purple Orchid *(Orchis mascula)*. By the sea there are carpets of Sea Pink *(Armeria maritima)*, white Sea Campion *(Silene maritima)*, bright yellow Bird's-foot Trefoil *(Lotus corniculatus)* and pale blue Spring Squill *(Scilla verna)*.

The basaltic scarps and glens extend from Benbradagh and Binevenagh in County Derry to Belfast. Tread softly on Binevenagh: it is a holy mountain for Irish botanists. Moss Campion *(Silene acaulis)* is there in profusion, with flowers of every shade from dark purple to white. Purple Saxifrage *(Saxifraga oppositifolia)* creeps in damp places; Mountain Avens *(Dryas octopetala)*, the elegant Hoary Whitlow Grass *(Draba incana)* and Common Milkwort *(Polygala Spp.)* are also there. The great Irish botanist Praeger found that certain plants, normally of maritime and lowland distribution in Ireland, occur here above the alpine species at heights over 1,000 feet.

On the basaltic plateaux, scarps and slopes you will find the very delicate, pale Vernal Sandwort *(Minuartia verna)* in a very few places; on high rocks the Mossy Saxifrage *(Saxifraga hypnoides)* is worth looking for; the Roseroot occurs in rocky crevices, as does Enchanter's Nightshade *(Circaea intermedia)*; in moist rocky places you can find Northern Bedstraw *(Galium boreale)* and yellow Marsh Hawk's Beard *(Crepis paludosa)*. Where there are high-level scrubby woods one can find *Orobanche rubra*, a blood-red Broomrape, and Wood Fescue *(Festuca sylvatica)* among the early-flowering Wych Elm *(Ulmus glabra)* and the rarer Aspen *(Populus tremula)*. On Knockdhu and Robin Young's Hill the Mountain Avens *(Dryas octopetala)* grows.

Locally in the glens will be found Rock Whitebeam *(Sorbus rupicola)* and Wood Cranesbill *(Geranium sylvaticum)*, with its reddish-purple flowers.

The Garron Plateau is a vast, lonely and beautiful wilderness; over much of it Heather *(Calluna vulgaris)* is dominant with two grasses — Purple Moor-grass *(Molinia caerulea)* and Deer Grass *(Tricophorum caespitosum)*. You can also find the very pretty mauve Bog Violet *(Viola palustris)* and the yellow Common Tormentil *(Potentilla erecta)* as well as a great variety of sedges. Both high up and low down is the tiny pinkish lilac flower of the Butterwort *(Pinguicula lusitanica)*. In wet places Yellow Mountain Saxifrage *(Saxifraga aizoides)* grows; and Great Sundew *(Drosera anglica)*; Bog-bean *(Menyanthes trifoliata)*; the blue-violet Self-heal *(Prunella vulgaris)* and Sharp-flowered Rush *(Juncus acutiflorus)*.

On the east Antrim shore, you will find the yellow Sea Radish *(Raphanus maritimus)* and Spring Vetch *(Vicia lathyroides)*; both are rare and confined to only a few sandy stretches. More frequent is the Seaside Pansy *(Viola tricolor* var. *curtisii)*, the Sea Pearlwort *(Sagina maritima)* and Rock Spurry *(Spergularia rupicola).* Locally abundant are Greater Hawk's Beard *(Crepis biennis)* and in shaded areas, Intermediate Enchanter's Nightshade *(Circaea intermedia).*

In the north-west of the region lies the great sandy triangle of Magilligan, perhaps best appreciated when first seen from the summit of Binevenagh. In the alternating series of dunes and slacks are many species, some rare, and many common; they include the Seaside Pansy, Spring Vetch, Northern Bedstraw *(Galium boreale);* yellow Smooth Cat's-ear *(Hypochoeris glabra);* the beautiful blushing Marsh Helleborine *(Epipactis palustris);* Spike-rush *(Eleocharis uniglumis);* Primrose; and Wild Strawberry *(Fragaria vesca).* The glory of Magilligan is at its greatest in the autumn when the Grass of Parnassus *(Parnassia palustris)* is still in bloom, its solitary, fragile, white flower with five clearly veined petals, and the Burnet Rose *(Rosa spinosissima)* is all purple and red from its berries and leaves. On nearby cliffs as well as on the dunes grow Hoary Whitlow Grass and Red Broomrape *(Orobanche rubra)* which is parasitic on Thyme *(Thymus drucei).* Among the introduced species are American Speedwell *(Veronica peregrina)* and the heath *Erica terminalis.*

In the Sperrins there is Starry Saxifrage; Cowberry; Least Willow; Lesser Twayblade *(Listera cordata),* an elegant and modest plant among the heather; Welsh Poppy; Marsh Hawk's Beard and Pink Butterwort. Among the rarities are the Wintergreens *(Pyrola media and P. minor);* Yellow Bartsia *(Parentucellia viscosa);* and on Dart Mountain the very rare Cloudberry *(Rubus chamaemorus),* with pretty dove-white flowers and amber fruit.

In Fermanagh a number of rare northern plants are seen on the limestone and the sandstone, the scarps of the latter being particularly rich. Abundantly on the limestones are Mossy Saxifrage; Narrow-leaved Eyebright *(Euphrasia salisburgensis);* Yew *(Taxus baccata);* and under the Hazel *(Corylus avellana),* Woodruff *(Galium odoratum)* is plentiful. Among the most interesting localities are Magho, a major limestone escarpment overlooking Lower Lough Erne, where you will find the prostrate Yellow Mountain Saxifrage, Roseroot, and the pretty mauve Bitter Vetch *(Lathyrus montanus);* the cliff and grassland area of Knockmore, which yields Mountain Avens, Juniper, and Broad-leaved Cotton-grass *(Eriophorum latifolium);* Monawilkin; and the wooded glen of Marble Arch.

On the sandstone scarps there are Welsh Poppy, three Wintergreens *(Pyrola media, P. minor and P. secunda),* Cowberry and Lesser Twayblade. Praeger pointed out that some lime-loving plants such as Blue Moor Grass *(Sesleria caerulea)* and Hairy Rock-cress *(Arabis hirsuta)* grow on the high sandstone scarps, far from limestone, and mix with markedly lime-avoiding species such as Heather *(Calluna vulgaris),* Bell Heather *(Erica cinera)* and Foxglove *(Digitalis purpurea).*

There are many expanses of bog in the west, which often include many *Sphagnum* species including *S. rubellum* and *S. fuscum;* and great hummocks of *Rhacomitrium lanuginosum* may be seen, separated by sinuous pools. Near Belcoo grow the only Irish plants of

Cornish Heath *(Erica vagans)*, here flowering white in August on a remote hillside.

Fauna The elegant Irish hare *(Lepus timidus hibernicus)*, a sub-species of the Arctic hare *(Lepus timidus)*, is probably the most obvious large mammal in the hills. Unlike its European counterpart *(Lepus timidus Europaeus)* it does not turn white in winter, but individuals sometimes show signs of white. The brown hare *(Lepus capensis)* occurs in the west of the province. The fox *(Vulpes vulpes)* is widespread and may occasionally be encountered even high up in the moors, while badgers *(Meles meles)* may be sought at nightfall near their setts in glens and old woodland. Smaller mammals such as wood mice *(Apodemus sylvaticus)* and pigmy shrews *(Sorex minutus)* take advantage of the cover provided by forestry plantations and can be found at quite high levels. They provide a source of food for kestrels. Where rabbits *(Oryctolagus cuniculus)* are plentiful, stoats *(Mustela erminea hibernica)*, much larger than those in Britain, may also be found. The pine marten *(Martes martes)* which lives in woodland areas has seldom been recorded. During the summer evenings pipistrelle *(Pipistrellus pipistrellus)* and long-eared bats *(Plecotus auritus)* hawk for insects in the gathering dusk along the edges of forests.

The most widespread bird in the uplands is probably the meadow pipit *(Anthus pratensis)* which is an important host species for the cuckoo *(Cuculus canorus)*. In spring its distinctive parachute display flight is a common sight. The wide open spaces provide an ideal habitat for the skylark *(Alauda arvensis)*, since it also does not require a song post. An attractive summer visitor, widespread in hill areas, is the wheatear *(Oenanthe oenanthe)*. During the spring and summer it may be seen flitting from rock to rock around the Hare's Gap or Pigeon Rock Mountain or on the moorland above Cushendall. The moist bog lands of North Antrim and the Sperrins, remote and featureless, are places where the walker may encounter the golden plover *(Charadrius apricarius)*. The tracts of heather, glorious in the months of August and September, provide sustenance and shelter for the red grouse *(Lagopus scoticus)*, but this species is nowhere abundant. The numerous hill streams invariably have their resident pairs of grey wagtails *(Motacilla cinerea)* and dippers *(Cinclus cinclus)*. The dipper nests under bridges and may be seen flitting from rock to rock carrying beakfuls of aquatic larvae to feed its young. In summer the shrill piping of the common sandpiper *(Tringa hypoleucos)* is a characteristic sound of the Antrim Plateau. In rough scrub areas of whin the linnet *(Carduelis cannabina)* breeds, while on the open moorland of North Antrim another seedeater, the twite *(Carduelis flavirostris)*, may sometimes be seen.

Many areas of afforestation provide, especially in the early stages, habitats for an increased range of species. The willow warbler's *(Phylloscopus trochilus)* silvery cadence and the 'spee-vee' call of the lesser redpoll *(Carduelis flammea cabaret)* are characteristic sounds of summer. Whinchats *(Saxicola rubetra)* are widespread summer visitors, nesting on the fringes of young forest areas. Goldcrests *(Regulus regulus)*, siskins *(Carduelis spinus)*, chaffinches *(Fringilla coelebs)*, wrens *(Troglodytes troglodytes)*, blackbirds *(Turdus merula)* all frequent the forest until it reaches a stage of maturity where it is attractive mainly to wood pigeons *(Columba palumbus)* and magpies *(Pica pica)*.

The moorland areas have predators adapted to their environment. The hen harrier *(Circus cyaneus)*, a scarce breeding species, may occasionally be seen quartering the open ground in search of food, while the diminutive merlin's *(Falco columbarius)* dashing flight in pursuit of meadow pipits and skylarks is an exhilarating sight. In the more remote areas the sickle shape of the peregrine falcon *(Falco peregrinus)* may be glimpsed. The golden eagle *(Aquila chrysaetos)* no longer breeds in Ulster, but in Antrim and north Derry the broad-winged buzzard *(Buteo buteo)* may be seen wheeling in easy circles over the moorland and glens. Kestrels *(Falco tinnunculus)* are widespread in most areas.

The walker in winter may find the birdlife less varied. In the Mournes and elsewhere the sonorous croak and sombre shape of the raven *(Corvus corax)*, the lone heron *(Ardea cinerea)* by the mountain stream, and the occasional mallard *(Anas platyrhincos)* and teal *(Anas crecca)* may add interest to a day's outing. The vast tracts of moorland with small pools which abound in Antrim, the Sperrins and Fermanagh may occasionally provide solitude and food for Greenland white-fronted geese *(Anser flavirostris)* and snipe *(Gallinago gallinago)*. Small parties of snow-buntings *(Plectrophenax nivalis)* and short-eared owls *(Asio flammeus)* may occur, particularly when winter conditions are severe elsewhere.

The scope of this book permits only a passing reference to the waterside birds and water birds that we can see on or near the shores of our coast, sea loughs and inland loughs. There are colonies of great-crested grebes *(Podiceps cristatus)* and numerous ducks, geese and swans *(Anatidae)* and coots *(Fulica atra)* in freshwater areas, while on the coast and in the estuaries and the sea-loughs you will find, in addition to various ducks, geese and swans, a myriad of waders, including curlews *(Numenius arquata)*, black-tailed godwits *(Limosa limosa)*, bar-tailed godwits *(L. lapponica)*, dunlin *(Calidris alpina)*, knot *(Calidris canutus)* and various plovers *(Charidriidae)*, as well as oyster-catchers *(Haematopus ostralegus)*, gannets *(Sula bassana)*, cormorants *(Phalacrocorax carbo)*, shags *(P. aristotelis)*, various gulls and terns *(Laridae)* and various auks *(Alcidae)*. The coastal walks that I describe will give opportunities to see many of these, and in the places where you stay short walks in the early morning may be even more productive.

Mountain Safety

The Ulster hills are still relatively unfrequented. This is a happy situation for the hill walker, except on the occasion when he does get into serious trouble and needs help, which may have to come from a considerable distance. It is therefore important to take all reasonable precautions.

1. Wear suitable clothing. Bring warm clothing, a wind- and water-

proof anorak, and for the higher walks, overtrousers. Except on short easy walks it is best to wear walking boots.

2. Plan your walk, and make sure you can complete it before dark. To estimate the time a walk will take, allow one hour for each three miles and add half an hour for each 750 ft of ascent. You may vary this rule to fit your own walking pace. Add time for viewing, photography and meals.

3. Check weather forecasts. Keep a lookout for weather changes. On high ground mist and rain can close in with alarming speed.

4. Remember that the temperature drops 2–3 °C. for each 1,000 ft you climb. If (as frequently happens) the wind is strong on the hills, the temperature drop will be even more marked. It may be a pleasant day at sea level when it is freezing and windy at 2,000 ft.

5. Carry a map, and if you are going high, a compass. Also a torch, a whistle and a small first-aid kit.

6. Carry a reserve supply of food – chocolate, glucose tablets.

7. Leave word of where you are going at your hotel, guest-house or youth hostel and say what time you expect to come back. If you park your car at the beginning of a walk, leave a note on the seat.

Obviously some of the precautions listed above are designed for the longer, higher walks, but do remember that, especially in winter, the Irish hills can be dangerous.

If your party does have an accident, dial 999 and ask for Mountain Rescue.

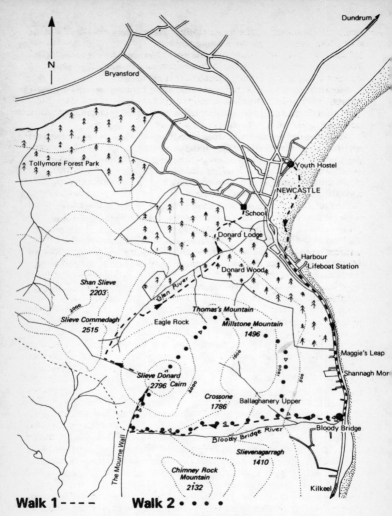

Walk 1 - - - - Walk 2 • • • •

1. SLIEVE DONARD FROM NEWCASTLE Y.H. Slieve Donard (2,796 ft) is the highest mountain in the nine counties of Ulster. It is not as attractive as the toothed Bearnach or the castellated Bignian, but its profile dominates the skyline for most visitors to County Down.

Through Down and Armagh the Mournes appear in the landscape in an ever-changing pattern that depends on the traveller's position and the atmosphere and light. They are by any standards a most attractive

16

group of mountains. They are compact: within an elliptical area of about fourteen miles by seven miles there are thirty-five summits over 1,500 feet. They roll down to the sea at two places – Newcastle and Rostrevor – and they contain in their valleys and foothills a lively and energetic people still actively engaged in farming.

Apart from the cultivated, outgoing valleys, old woodlands and new forests, the Mournes supply a scant pasture for sheep on the lesser hills, but in the centre all is wilderness and so a much-loved habitat for the walker.

Walk south for one mile along the Newcastle shore to the harbour or, if the tide is in, you may go by the promenade. The forest of Donard Park which rises on the slopes of the mountain from the edge of the town is the former estate of the Earls of Annesley. Newcastle got its name from a castle of the Magennis family which stood at the south of the Shimna. Near the site are the municipal offices in a pavilion-type building (badly damaged by bombs) originally the bath-house. It is a single-storey building of ashlar granite with six Doric columns, a hipped roof and Georgian glazed windows.

In the promenade gardens there is a fountain commemorating Percy French (1854–1920) who wrote and composed 'The Mountains of Mourne' and many other songs such as 'Are you right there, Michael?', 'Phil the Fluter's Ball' and 'Slattery's Mounted Fut', as well as capturing the Irish landscape in atmospheric water-colours.

Continue along the coast road for one mile to Maggie's Leap. This is a narrow chasm 370 feet deep which Maggie on her way to market jumped to escape from an unwanted suitor. It is a volcanic extrusion washed out from harder rocks by the sea. Along this stretch of coast the sea has eaten into the baked grits, and the low cliffs, hung with maritime plants, are tunnelled here and there by caves (accessible only from the sea) such as Donard's Cave, connected traditionally with St Domangard, and Armor's Hole which tradition associates with the murder of James Armor by his son in 1701. (The hole is now almost filled in.)

Continue for a mile to Bloody Bridge. Opposite the car park take the National Trust path that leads past a sheep pen over springy ground between granite boulders along the north side of the Bloody Bridge River. On the left is the old bridge, the scene of a massacre in 1641, from which the bridge and river take their name. Here a number of Protestants of Newry with their minister were killed in the troubled year 1641 at the instigation of Sir Conn Magennis. The whin (gorse) growing in the thin soil is brilliant here and the sheep nibble its young flowers. Bog myrtle and heather add their scent to that of the whin and the river tumbles downwards in a series of cascades and deep green pools. As W. R. Rodgers said:

... There was Bloody River
Where the granite prickles bristled and blazed, and
Ebullient water bellied over
Boulders with the sweep of a bell's shoulders,
And pancaked out in pools.

The Bloody Bridge Youth Hostel on the left at 500 ft was entirely built by the early members of the Youth Hostel Association of Northern Ireland in 1933/34; it is no longer used as a hostel.

Climb past the granite quarry. This granite is very much part of Ulster. Belfast's streets were paved with granite square-sets and Stormont's Parliament Buildings are based on a foundation of Mourne granite. The path here is worn by the boots of quarrymen and of hikers.

Climb to the col between Donard and Chimney Rock. Here you will meet the massive wall of granite built in the days before and after the First World War by the Belfast Water Commissioners to define their catchment area. The wall runs over the tops of fifteen mountains and encloses about 9,000 acres. The work was started in 1910 and completed in 1922. The Mourne workmen walked to work every day and as the wall progressed their walks were longer. The stones were all quarried on the mountains. The wall is on average five feet high and between two and a half and three feet at the base, tapering slightly towards the top; cement was not used except at a few difficult places.

Follow the wall (or walk on top of it) to the top of Donard. This mountain of St Domangard is a massive lump and lacks crags except on its northern side where it overlooks the Glen River on the 1,500 contour. Of two ruined cairns 800 ft apart the one on the summit cannot be distinguished. The other at 2,720 ft to the north-east, though mutilated, survives.

The Annals of the Four Masters, under Anno Mundi, 2,533, has an entry: "Slainge, son of Partholan, died in this year, and was interred in the carn on Slibh Slanga". The mountain was for many centuries called by this name. The mountain and the cairn were associated with St Domangard (Donard), a 5th-century follower of Patrick who built a monastery at Maghera, four miles to the north. The cairn was a place of pilgrimage in Colgan's time (1645).

The view from the top is very fine, and includes the hills of the Isle of Man, the mountains of Cumberland and south-west Scotland and the Hill of Howth.

Follow down the wall north-west to the col between Donard and Commedagh, then drop north-east with, on your left, the Pot of Pulgarve (where you should hear the raven's pruck) and follow the track along the Glen River until you come to the stile into Donard Lodge Plantation. There are various paths through the woods to Newcastle.

Distance: 10 miles.   Ascent: 2,700 ft.   Walking Time: 5 hours.

2. SLIEVE DONARD FROM BLOODY BRIDGE   Take your car to the Bloody Bridge car park (J 390 270). Follow the route of Walk No. 1 to the top of Donard. From Donard drop down north-east along the gradual descent in the direction of Newcastle to Thomas's Mountain, a lumpy foothill of Donard, with a cap of baked slate-rocks lying on the granite. From Thomas's turn south-east for Millstone (1,496 ft). Then drop to the "Pipeline" (which brings the Mourne water to Belfast). The Pipeline is distinguished, about the 700 ft contour, by small, usually black, gates in the occasional stone walls which mark off the mountain

pastures. Continue due south, at the line of the pipeline, until you meet the Bloody Bridge River; then drop down to the car park.

Distance: 7 miles.   Ascent: 2,800 ft.   Walking Time: 4¼ hours.

3. NEWCASTLE Y.H. TO SLIEVENAMAN Y.H. Walk up through the Donard Lodge Plantation along the Glen River until you reach a wall at the end of the planting, and climb over the stile. Continue on the track along the river south-west for 1¼ miles. Cross to the west side of the river and continue south-west along it. The Pot of Pulgarve (*poll garbh*, rough pool) and the precipitous slopes of Commedagh are on your right. Climb to the col between Slieve Commedagh (*sliabh coimheada*, the Mountain of Watching) and Donard. Climb west up Commedagh (2,515 ft), avoiding the steep east side. Shan Slieve (*sen sliabh*, the Old Mountain; 2,203 ft) makes an easy but interesting addition. From Commedagh follow the wall over Slieve Corragh and Slievenaglogh (Mountain of the Goats) to the Hare's Gap. An alternative to climbing the peaks from the Commedagh/Donard col is to drop to the Brandy Pad – a former way for smuggling alcohol inland from the ports of Annalong and Kilkeel. This path keeps between the 1,500 and 1,750 contours to the Hare's Gap and passes the weathered granite bastions and pillars known as the Castles. Here a series of vertical and horizontal joints traverse the rock which is very slowly being disintegrated by wind and rain. A short climb from the path will bring you to the Diamond Rocks which lie on the south slope of Slievenaglogh, 700 yards from the Hare's Gap and 300 ft above it. These rocks are drusy cavities – crystal-filled bubbles – in the granite into which minerals have infiltrated to form crystals of smoky quartz, orthoclase, black mika, topaz and beryl.

From the Hare's Gap follow the path along the Trassey Burn, mainly on the east side. Cross to the west of the river, and from the minor road use the footbridge to cross the Shimna River 400 yards upstream from the hostel.

Distance: 7 miles. Ascent: 2,700 ft (by Brandy Pad, 1,900 ft). Walking Time: 4¼ hours (3½ by Brandy Pad).

4. SLIEVE BEARNAGH FROM SLIEVENAMAN Y.H. Cross the Shimna River by the footbridge upstream from the hostel. Follow the track by the Trassey Burn. The ascent is fairly steep till you reach the Spellack (*speilic*, a splintery rock), a spur of Slieve Meelmore which overhangs the valley in a towering precipice. The Hare's Gap is straight in front, with a low cliff overhanging it on either side. The stream flows through long pools where tiny trout may be seen darting over the white granite sand. A glen with precipitous sides between Bearnagh and Meelmore now opens to the right; the slope of Meelmore is particularly steep on the right flank of the glen. Climb to the Hare's Gap (1,300 ft). This is a notable gap, for it is a kind of grand entrance to the Mournes. As you reach it and cross the wall you have before you the head of the Kilkeel River – a wilderness of brown bog with the green dome of Donard towering on the left above the lower mountains – Commedagh,

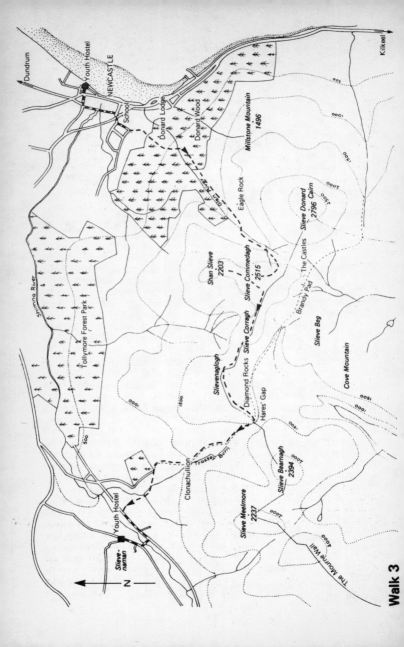

Walk 3

Slieve Beg, Cove, Lamagan and Bignian. It is a gateway to the wilderness. Spellack hangs over the valley up which you have come and the placid checkered fields of Down lie spread, with Lough Island Reavey reflecting the sky.

Facing to the right keep round a precipitous escarpment with a flat top and bushes of dwarf juniper. There is now a comparatively smooth but steep slope to the top of Bearnagh (*sliabh bernach*, gapped mountain). Alpine club-moss and dwarf willow grow among the scant turf. The summit is crowned with gigantic granite rocks and from the topmost pinnacle there are spectacular views on every side. This is a fine place for lunch as it is usually possible to get out of the wind on one side or other of a pinnacle.

In her book, *The Mountains of Ireland*, Dr Pochin Mould gives a vivid account of how she saw the Spectre of the Brocken from the top of Bearnagh. She had climbed the mountain from the Hare's Gap and, with the sun behind her, looked across the glen below the ridge of Bearnagh to the opposite slope of Meelmore which was still veiled in cloud.

This phenomenon is the enormously magnified shadow of the observer cast upon a bank of cloud in high mountain regions when the sun is low. The shadow, often accompanied by coloured bands, reproduces every motion of the observer in the form of a gigantic but misty image of himself. It is so named from having been observed in 1780 on the Brocken, the highest point of the Harz Mountains in Saxony.

Strange things have been seen in the mists of Irish mountains. In *Cronicum Scotorum* we read of horse-riders on a mountain in Eirann passing on the clouds in January, 851 A.D. William Leyburn in his book, *The Whole Art of Optics*, published in 1724, speaks of "the ghosts of Brocken", but no doubt the 1780 observation was more exact. Dr Edgar, in the *Irish Mirror* of 1805, tells of something like the Brocken Spectre having been seen on Slieve Donard in 1795. Lieut Murphy, R.E., of the Ordnance Survey, writing to Drummond in 1825, relates that he and his company, passing up Slieve Snaght, in Co. Donegal, were 'shadowed in the clouds". (See also under Walk 12.)

From Bearnagh walk down west to the col (1,700 ft) between that mountain and Meelmore. At the col turn a little to the right up the slope of Meelmore (*Sliabh mael-mór*, the big bare mountain). Near the summit there is a vein of amethyst sparkling purple in the granite. The mountain is 2,237 ft and thus lower than Meelbeg (*Sliabh mael-beg*, the little bare mountain; 2,310 ft). This seems strange, but is probably accounted for by the bigger, stouter appearance of Meelmore when seen from the valleys below; bigness is not merely height. From Meelmore climb down into the hollow and up Meelbeg. You may be tempted to cut short the walk by returning north down Meelmore or Meelbeg, but the way down both these routes is long and arduous and Meelbeg to the north-west is very precipitous. Instead go down south-west towards Slieve Loughshannagh; climb this mountain (called after the long lake on its south side, the lake of the foxes) and here again there is a new and rewarding view.

From here it is an easy climb to Ott (1,724 ft). Go down by the track on its north-west flank to the road that runs north out of the Deer's Meadow. And so back to the hostel past the reservoir and the coniferous woods.

Distance: 9 miles.   Ascent: 3,050 ft.   Walking Time: 5 hours.

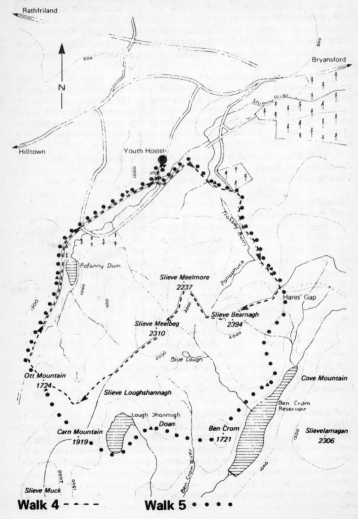

Walk 4 - - - -   Walk 5 • • • •

5. BEN CROM, DOAN, CARN FROM SLIEVENAMAN Y.H.

Having climbed the peaks of the outer horseshoe of the Mournes, it is worthwhile to explore the smaller hills in the interior.

Climb to Hare's Gap and make south-west across the heathery plateau (1,500—1,700 ft) of Bearnagh, through great worn stacks of peat and the grit of weathered granite. Cross a stream and climb south to Ben Crom (the stooped mountain, 1,721 ft). It is especially attractive because, like Bearnagh and Bignian, it has a hard craggy face; indeed it has a sheer drop down to the Ben Crom reservoir. From below it is like a mountain split in half, for it is intersected by a great dyke of porphyritic felstone.

From the top drop west across the Ben Crom River which pours down south into the Silent Valley. Climb Doan (2,000 ft), the Hook, a pointed mountain from which you obtain another inner view of the mountains. From here Lough Shannagh, an attractive lake with worn granite sand, lies between you and Carn (1,919 ft). The little stream to the south-west which flows into the Spelga Dam is the source of the great River Bann which divides Northern Ireland in two and you may follow it, but it would be easier to make for Ott (1,724 ft) and follow the track from it down to the road.

Distance: 9 miles.   Ascent: 2,600 ft.   Walking Time: 4¾ hours.

6. HEN, COCK AND ROCKY MOUNTAINS, PIERCE'S CASTLE FROM KINNAHALLA Y.H.

These are small but interesting mountains and provide a very pleasant day's walking. Cross the Bann River and climb Hen (1,189 ft), a craggy mountain like a miniature Bignian with some good pitches on which to practise rock-climbing. Drop down south-east and climb Cock (1,666 ft). In the valley between Cock and Rocky there are three streams: Rocky Water, Rowan Tree River and one un-named, all delectable for bathing the feet on a hot day. Climb Rocky (1,326 ft) and from there go south along the ridge to Pierce's Castle, a great boss of granite. Follow the path down north-west to near Leitrim Lodge and take the right fork for home. Leitrim Lodge was formerly a Youth Hostel, much loved by early members of the Youth Hostel Association of Northern Ireland. As you approach the Kinnahalla hostel in the month of June, the hillside is a blaze of purple. The old woodland here was felled many years ago, but the rhododendrons flourish in the cleared peaty ground.

Distance: 7 miles.   Ascent: 2,200 ft.   Walking time: 3¾ hours.

7. PIGEON ROCK, SLIEVEMOUGHANMORE, EAGLE MOUNTAIN, SHANLIEVE FROM KINNAHALLA Y.H.

Take the Kilkeel road past the Spelga Dam and through the Deer's Meadow. Just as the Happy Valley had to give way to the Silent Valley Reservoir when it was completed in 1932, so the Deer's Meadow had to become substantially occupied by the Spelga Dam in 1957. The Deer's Meadow is a near plain of bog-covered land, about two square miles in extent, surrounded by green hills. It gets its name from the red deer which formerly grazed here. To these pastures, in the 18th century and probably also in the

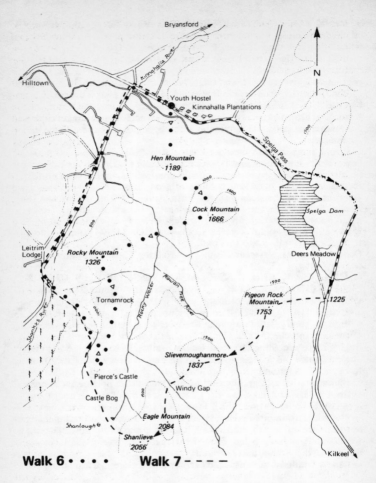

Bryansford

Hilltown

Youth Hostel

Kinnahalla Plantations

Spelga Pass

Hen Mountain
1189

Cock Mountain
1666

Spelga Dam

Leitrim Lodge

Deers Meadow

Rocky Mountain
1326

Tornamrock

Pigeon Rock Mountain
1753

1225

Slievemoughanmore
1837

Pierce's Castle

Windy Gap

Castle Bog

Shanlough

Eagle Mountain
2084

Shanlieve
2056

Kilkeel

N

Walk 6 • • • •   Walk 7 - - - -

19th, herds of cattle were driven in the summer from the northern low-lands. This practice was called booleying and traces of booley huts have been found. In his *Antient and Present State of the County of Down* (1744) Harris wrote that the Mourne Mountains "give pasture to a great number of cattle in the summer, being commons to the adjacent parts of the county. In the bosom of the Mourne Mountains there is a place called the Deer's Meadow, and by some, the King's Meadow (because people have their grazing in it free) extending some miles in breadth and length; to which great numbers of poor people resort in the summer months to graze their cattle. They bring with them their wives, children and little wretched furniture, erect huts, and there live for two months, and sometimes more, and often cut their turf to serve for the next returning season; which done, they retire with their cattle to their former habitations".

Leave the road at about the 1,225 ft mark on the one-inch map, and climb Pigeon Rock (1,753 ft), called after the rock pigeons which favour it. The cliffs of this mountain give an insight into the history of the local rocks. The oldest beds are the crumpled and metamorphosed Ordovician grits, which may be seen capping the granite. The grits are penetrated by a series of basalt dykes, newer than the grits, since they cut through them, but older than the granite, since they are cut off abruptly at its margin. Next in order comes the granite itself, which has carried up on its surface the old sedimentary rocks of Ordovician times. Finally since the cooling of the granite fresh eruptions have taken place, for a second set of basaltic dykes is seen which cuts through both the granite and the grits.

From the summit, a broad expanse of springy moorland, it is a natural progression to climb Slievemoughanmore (1,837 ft), Eagle Mountain (2,084 ft) and Shanlieve (Old Mountain; 2,056 ft).

Eagle Mountain has a most commanding view of the valley of the White Water, with its patchwork of fields and white houses, down to Kilkeel and the coast. Eagle has a towering precipice which has attracted the peregrine falcon from time to time. The cliff is decked with flowers and grasses, and ferns flourish in the shady nooks. The tiny filmy fern clothes the rocks with dense mats of wiry rhizomes and dark green fronds. On the ledges and at the base of the cliffs the great woodrush grows luxuriantly.

From Shanlieve cross west-north-west past the tiny Shanlough and through the Castle Bog to Pierce's Castle and so to the road near Leitrim Lodge. Take the right fork for home.

Distance: 10½ miles.   Ascent: 2,750 ft.   Walking Time: 5¼ hours.

8. SLIEVE BIGNIAN
This is such an interesting mountain that it is best to climb it on its own, though it is also included in the Inner Horseshoe (Walk 9). A road running east-west skirts the Mournes on the south side and passes the wooded entrance to the Silent Valley (formerly the Happy Valley). Leave your car two-thirds of a mile east of the entrance and take the track going north (J 319 209). A small hill called Moolieve (1,092 ft) appears before you. It should be climbed as the view is very fine and it gives you a gradual approach to Bignian along its south-west shoulder. Just above the 1,250 ft contour is a craggy foothill, Wee Bignian, which you should also climb. Towards the top of Bignian the going is steep and at the top there are magnificent weathered pillars of granite. These are grouped along the top for half a mile and you can usually find a place out of the wind for refreshments. Bignian is central to the great horseshoe of the Mourne peaks, so it is a fine place for identifying the landscape. The ridge over the 2,000 ft contour is more than a mile long and provides an exhilarating walk with chang-

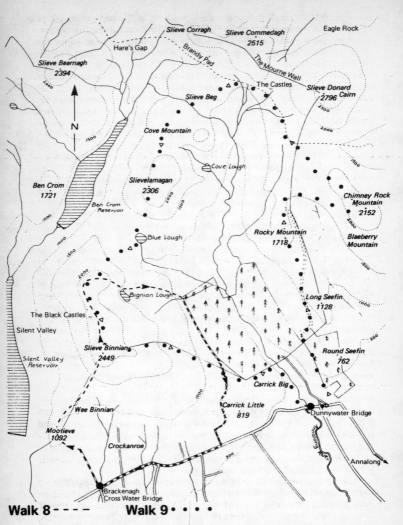

Walk 8 - - - -   Walk 9 • • • •

ing views. At the northern end of the ridge drop down east to Bignian Lough and continue east till you come to the track which will lead you south to the road which connects with the east-west road at Carrick Little. This is 1¾ miles east of your starting-point.

Distance: 7 miles.   Ascent: 1,900 ft.   Walking Time: 3½ hours.

9. THE INNER HORSESHOE Park your car at Dunnywater Bridge over the Annalong River (J 354 223). Walk east and take the second track on your left; this will lead you north towards Rocky Mountain, and a minor track will take you almost to the top (1,718 ft). Go north in the direction of Donard, but after half a mile turn east and climb Chimney Rock (2,152 ft), scrambling over the granite tors which crown it. Go down north-west to the col and along the Brandy Pad towards the Castles of Commedagh. On your left is the Annalong Valley (to be avoided because of its difficult terrain – huge granite boulders, bog and hidden holes). Opposite you is the steep face of Slieve Beg, split from top to bottom by the chasm called the Devil's Coach-road'. Looking down the Annalong Valley you now have the crags of Beg, Cove, Lamagan and Bignian on your right. At the southern end of a cliff of Cove there is a long cave which opens through a spur of rock to the mountainside behind, but the passage is almost closed by large fallen granite blocks. Both the lough and the mountain are named from the cave. You will climb Beg, Cove and Lamagan without descending much below 1,750 ft.

The calm, round tarn, Blue Lough, is below you at 1,100 ft and the descent to it is steep and rocky. From Blue Lough climb south-west up the north end of Bignian, whence you will look down on Bignian Lough. It is a mile of springy walking along the top of Bignian with tors and crags and ever-changing views, finally coming to the peak (2,449 ft) and its dramatic view of the fields and white houses of the Kingdom of Mourne, spread out between their stone walls towards the sea at Anna-long and Kilkeel.

From Bignian and from the map you will see a number of ways of returning to Dunnywater Bridge. Which one you take will depend on how much road walking you want at the end of a strenuous walk. If you want to stay on the mountain, follow the wall and come down by the Annalong River.

Distance: 13 miles. Ascent: 4,350 ft. Walking Time: 7¼ hours.

10. FINLIEVE This mountain is very little climbed, because of its isolation, its lack of any dramatic quality, and its small height (1,889 ft). But its great long hulk and its isolation should present a challenge to anyone who has climbed all the better-known peaks. Since much of the going is soft you should climb it in dry weather, preferably in May or June when the larks are rising in full song and the shy meadow pipit will try to divert you from its nest.

Take the main road from Kilkeel to Rostrevor to a point just east of the Lisnacree Post Office. Here a road runs due north straight for Fin-lieve through the townland of Glenloughan. Follow this for exactly one mile. At this point it swings to the right, leaving a space for parking at the foot of the Finlieve track (J 252 172). Park here and climb the track north-north-west. About half a mile up, just to the left of the track, there is a spring of pure, very cold water, known as the Slieveroe Well. The track runs for just over a mile, and then peters out in the bog, but there are two minor tracks. The one to the right goes into the Red

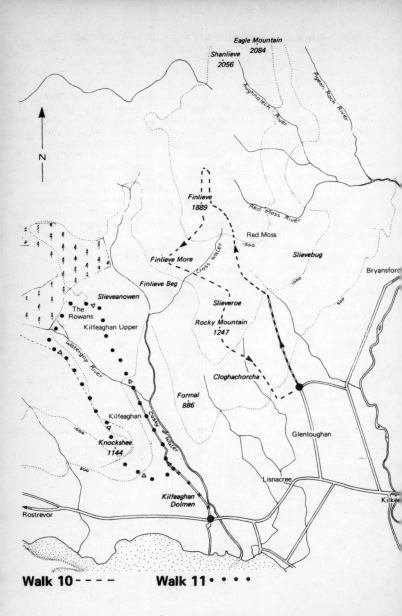

Eagle Mountain
2084

Shanlieve
2056

Aughnaleck River

Pigeon Rock River

Finlieve
1889

Red Moss River

Red Moss
1500

Slievebug

Bryansfor

Finlieve More

Cross Water

Finlieve Beg

Slieveanowen

The Rowans

Kilfeaghan Upper

Slieveroe

Rocky Mountain
1247

1000

500

Cloghachorcha

Watergap River

Formal
886

Glenloughan

Kilfeaghan

Cassy Water

Knockshee
1144

1000

500

Lisnacree

Kilfeaghan
Dolmen

Kilkee

Rostrevor

Walk 10 - - - -   **Walk 11** • • •

28

Moss, a peat bog where some turf-cutting is still done. The more direct route to the top of Finlieve is to follow the left-hand track which avoids much of the bog. The top of Finlieve is 1½ miles long to the top of Shanlieve (Walk No. 7); you may explore it for half a mile and return south. From Finlieve you have fine views of Carlingford Lough and the Carlingford Mountains and these will still be in sight as you drop down south-west to Finlieve More. Turn south-east across the Cross Water and then south, climbing over the top of Slieveroe and Rocky Mountain (1,247 ft). Make for the track running south-east on the left-hand side of the stream. At the 400 ft contour you will find a track going east on your left that will bring you the few hundred yards to your starting-point.

Distance: 6½ miles.   Ascent: 1,700 ft.   Walking Time: $3\frac{1}{3}$ hours.

11. THE KILFEAGHAN VALLEY

11. THE KILFEAGHAN VALLEY   You may either leave your car on the main road at the foot of the Kilfeaghan valley or drive it slowly northwards up the improved road which commences just west of the bridge over the Cassy Water (J 236 149). If you take the latter course you will park after 1¾ miles, up at the point where the tarmac ceases and a rough track continues (J 225 173). Go slowly, because the road, though smooth, is very narrow and the inhabited houses are very near.

This little valley is typical of the intense cultivation of hill land in some parts of Ireland; it is still thickly populated and reminds one very much of similar communities in County Donegal.

Many years ago I saw a woman here with twenty-two goats and it made me think that this might be one of the places to which Harris referred in Chapter X of his *Antient and Present State of the County of Down* (1744): "The Mountains of Mourne have been some years in repute for the benefit of goat's whey successfully prescribed by phisitians in scorbutick and nephritick ailments, as well as disorders in the lungs, being mostly ferquented in the spring and summer months, when the shrubs and medicinal herbs, with which these mountains abound, are in their greatest vigour, and afford the fittest nourishment to the goats; one of which here yields more profit in summer to the owner, than a milch cow in the same place. . . . Some have said, that these mountains bear a resemblance to the Alps, not so much in the height as the herbage, and that there, as with us, goat's milk and whey are in use for the same purposes. . . . It is drank in the months of April, May and June in large quantities, like the mineral waters, as from one pint to 8 or 9 in a morning, and its operation, like theirs, is various, . . . but as it retains something of the native balsam of the milk, when to prescribe the one or the other is the province of the phisitian".

Two fields in on the left of the access road is the Kilfeaghan Dolmen, at an altitude of 200 ft. It is a portal-grave, built of granite. The capstone, which weighs about thirty-five tons, may be a pre-existing erratic boulder, undermined to serve as a roofing-stone. A low cairn survives around the chamber and continues south for over eighty feet.

Follow the track northwards up to the east of the Rowans; then climb this small hill and go down south-west and cross the little Watergap River. Continue south-west until you come to an old turf-track and follow it south-east towards Knockshee, the Hill of the Fairies (1,144 ft). At the top of this small conical hill there is a round Bronze Age cairn apparently undisturbed except for the building of a small marker cairn on top of it. Here you are at the western end of the Kingdom of Mourne, that triangle of low land that lies between the two places where the Mountains of Mourne do roll down to the sea, one here at Carlingford Lough and the other at Bloody Bridge. From Knockshee drop down steeply to the narrow road and return to the car.

Distance: 5 miles (8½ miles if parking on main road). Ascent: 1,000 ft (1,350 ft if parking on main road). Walking Time: 2 hours, excluding Kilfeaghan Dolmen (3½ hours if parking on main road).

12. SLIEVEMEEN AND SLIEVE MARTIN
These hills overlooking Carlingford Lough provide something different from the rest of the Mournes: they see the very beautiful fiord in a great variety of moods; and their valleys are mild in climate and in places rich in undergrowth with plenty of cover for a great variety of small passerine birds.

Start your walk from the point shown on the map on the inner road above Killowen (J 204 155). Walk northwards up the lane which skirts the left side of Ballyedmond Wood to about the 500 ft contour and then follow the shoulder round north-west to the top of Spelga (1,322 ft). Here you will already have a fine view of the lough.

Continue northwards up Slievemeen (over 1500 ft). If you have started early in the morning on a fine day you may have the sight of rolling mists rising from the lough, clothing the lands opposite for a while and then clearing, with the sun coming strongly through over the entrance to the lough. Greencastle with its low lands will emerge on one side, and Greenore on the other, and then the giant serrated length of Slieve Foye and the rolling Cooley hills.

There is a record in the *Belfast Newsletter* of the Spectre of the Brocken having been seen on Slieve Martin during the Second World War by two men, one a United States soldier. Mist was lying in strata on Slieve Foye. "It was when we turned to look into the mist-filled glen above Rostrevor that we saw the Spectre. The sun was climbing over the low hills to the east of us, for we were now on the highest peak of the southern Mournes. It was difficult to think that those gigantic shadows, surrounded by a band of the prismatic colours, were thrown by our comparatively small selves. However, when we raised our hands, so did the spectre; when we took off our hats and waved them, so did the shadows; and when my friend held up his hand with fingers outstretched I wondered if it was the first time a Victory sign had been made by the Brocken Spectre over the tribal battleground of the southern Mournes." (See also Walk 4.)

Climb north to Slieve Martin (1,597 ft) where the Spectre was sighted, just outside the Rostrevor Forest. Then go east on your return journey round Slieve Fadda, dropping down to an old track that runs down the valley of the Ballincurry River. This track continues south-east on the east side of the river with the bracken-wreathed Knockshee on your

30

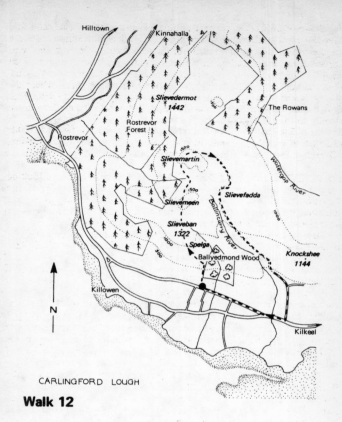

Walk 12

left. The track becomes completely overgrown, very bushy and alive with small birds.

When you reach the south-west side of Knockshee the track enters a lane which runs straight south for nearly half a mile past a large farm to the main road. Turn west for one mile to return to the starting-point.
Distance: 5 miles.   Ascent: 1,600 ft.   Walking Time: 2¾ hours.

13. ROSTREVOR TO KINNAHALLA Y.H. The old, lower and very beautiful wood is native and is of sessile oak; it is designated as a National Nature Reserve and is associated with a traditional walk up to the Fiddler's Green and the Cloghmore Stone. Ash, holly, hazel and wild cherry also thrive here in the soil which is derived from Silurian rocks.

The Cloghmore, the big stone, said by legend to have been thrown

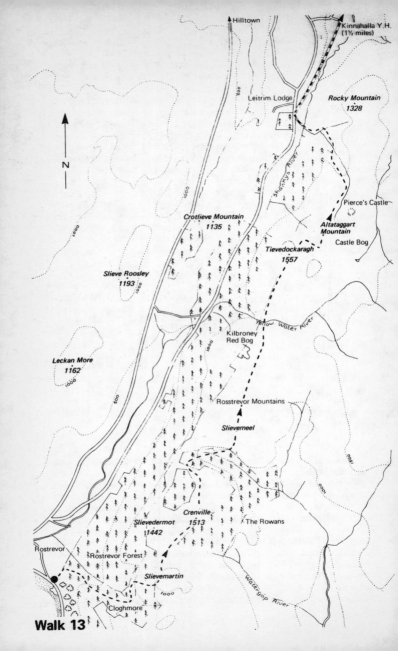

Hilltown

Kinnahalla Y.H.
(1½ miles)

Leitrim Lodge

Rocky Mountain
1328

Shanky's River

Pierce's Castle

Altataggart
Mountain

Crotlieve Mountain
1135

Castle Bog

Tievedockaragh
1557

Slieve Roosley
1193

Yellow Water River

Kilbroney
Red Bog

Leckan More
1162

Rosstrevor Mountains

Slievemeel

Crenville
1513

Slievedermot
1442

The Rowans

Rostrevor

Rostrevor Forest

Slievemartin

Watergap River

Cloghmore

Walk 13

across the Lough by the giant Finn at a rival giant on the Mournes, is in fact an enormous erratic brought here by the retreating ice.

The forest which now stretches north for several miles is planted with a variety of species which give it a varied attraction at different seasons. There are Douglas and Noble Fir; Lodgepole and Scots Pine; Sitka and Norway Spruce; and European and Japanese Larch. There are also some Western Red Cedar (Thuja) the bark of which, when older, scales off showing red underneath. There is also the graceful Western Hemlock (Tsuga) with its lace-work of pendent branches.

Walk up through the Nature Reserve to the Fiddler's Green and the Cloghmore. Continue from here to the car park and thence follow the sign-posted path to near the top of Slieve Martin. Leave the forest and climb to the top (1,597 ft).

Continue north over the moors, rich in heather and bilberries, to Crenville (1,513 ft) and past the woods to Slievemeel. Continue north-north-east over Kilbroney Red Bog. Cross the Yellow Water River and follow the track over Tievedockaragh (1,557 ft). Follow the old turf track between the woods and Pierce's Castle down to the road near Leitrim Lodge. Take the right fork for Kinnahalla Y.H.

Distance: 11 miles.   Ascent: 2,300 ft.   Walking Time: 5 hours.

14. THE COOLEY HILLS
These heathery, boggy mountains are only of moderate height, but the country is rich in folklore. It is the scene of much of the Cuchulain saga, though there are few traces left to-day of any memory of Cuchulain, who walked these hills 2,000 years ago.

There is a renowned view of Carlingford Lough from the Flagstaff, though you will get even better views if you take the walk described here. Leave your car at the Flagstaff (J 105 202), and walk along the road south-west to the Clontygora Horned Cairn. This is a three-chambered single-court grave known locally as the King's Ring. The court, 25 ft across, has two tall orthostats flanking the portal stones. Its excavation in 1937 yielded neolithic bowls, scrapers and an axe. Two hundred yards to the south is a smaller court-grave with one remaining chamber set in a long cairn.

Climb Anglesea Mountain (1,353 ft). You are actually standing on the Border here. Continue on it along the ridge to Clermont (1,465 ft). Going south along the ridge you are now in County Louth and over-looking the lovely Ravensdale valley. Continue south to Clermont Carn (1,674 ft). Drop south-east towards Carnavaddy (1,568 ft). Crossing your path is the Cadgers' Pad, a path which was the route of the herring-sellers who in the late nineteenth century came from Omeath with their donkeys, carrying creels of fish. You may take this path down the valley through Tullaghomeath, but I suggest you continue to the top of Carnavaddy where you will have further views of the Cooley peninsula. From here drop down to the Windy Gap and the site of the Long Woman's Grave (660 ft; see Walk No. 15). Return by Clermontpass Bridge, Lislea and Cornamucklagh. Although this is a long walk by road, it offers a variety of fine views, some conversation and very little traffic.

Distance: 11½ miles.   Ascent: 1,400 ft.   Walking Time: 4½ hours.

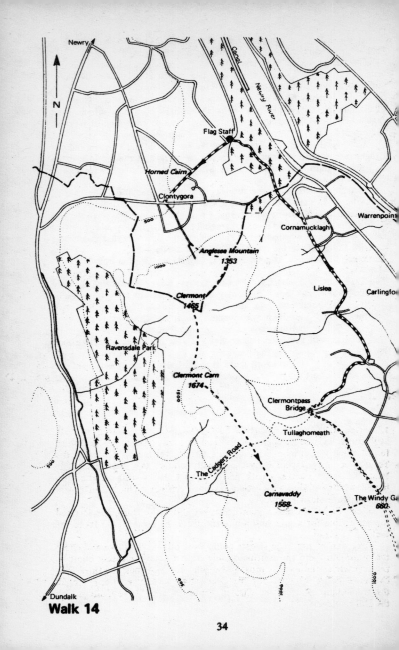

Newry

N

Flag Staff

Horned Cairn

Clontygora

Warrenpoint

Cornamucklagh

Anglesea Mountain
1353

Lislea

Carlingfo

Clermont
1465

Clermont Cairn
1674

Ravensdale Park

Clermontpass
Bridge

Tullaghomeath

The Cadgers Road

Carnavaddy
1568

The Windy Ga
660

Dundalk

Walk 14

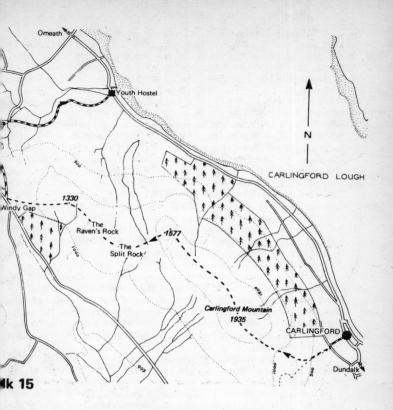

Omeath

Youth Hostel

CARLINGFORD LOUGH

N

1330

Windy Gap

The
Raven's Rock

1577

The
Split Rock

Carlingford Mountain
1935

CARLINGFORD

Dundalk

15. SLIEVE FOYE (CARLINGFORD MOUNTAIN)   Start your walk
in Carlingford, one of the most interesting small Irish towns, a Danish
foundation. It contains King John's Castle (thirteenth century); the
Tholsel or Corporation House, originally one of the town gates; the
Mint (fifteenth century) with pre-Norman Celtic motifs on the mul-
lioned windows; Taaffe's Castle (sixteenth century); and a fourteenth-
century Dominican Friary.

Slieve Foye lies like a giant, sleeping above the fiord, the serrated
top stretching for a mile and a quarter, from the head (1,935 ft) to the
toe (1,577 ft).

Take one of the little streets going west out of the town and climb
the mountain from the south-east side. It is a steady, pleasant climb to
the top where the view is most rewarding: the Mournes; the fiord with
Greenore Point reaching out for Greencastle on the northern side; all
the Cuchulain country, the Cooley Peninsula and Slieve Gullion; and
the Hill of Howth.

35

Walk along the ridge to the toe (1,577 ft) and then go west to the Split Rock and the Raven's Rock. Continue over a small hill (1,330 ft) and drop down to the Windy Gap and the site of the Long Woman's Grave. The grave was a megalithic chamber, but was destroyed by the road makers when they drove this road through the Gap. One Lorcan O'Hanlon, who came from this hollow in the hills, is said to have sought the hand of a very tall and beautiful Spanish lady called Cathleen. He told her that back in Ireland he could stand on a mountain from which everything he could see was his own. She consented to marry him and when he brought her to Ireland he took her here and showed her the rocks all around. She dropped dead on the spot and he buried her here, the place ever since being known as the Long Woman's Grave. Take the right-hand fork for Omeath. There is Youth Hostel at Ballinteskin, Omeath. (Information from An Oige, 39 Mountjoy Square, Dublin 1). There are two small hotels in Carlingford.

Distance: 7 miles.   Ascent: 2,050 ft.   Walking Time: $3\frac{2}{3}$ hours.

16. CAMLOUGH MOUNTAIN
Although this mountain could be climbed along with Slieve Gullion as part of a day's walking, it is better to make it a separate walk to allow more time for the exploration of both mountains.

From the village of Camlough drive south until you overlook Camlough lake at a fork where a by-road skirts the northern side of the mountain. Leave your car at this fork in the road at J 036 248. The view of the Crooked Lake from here is very fine, as some woodland on a promontory reaches out into the water and the old dark Scots pine contrasts with the gold of new Japanese larch in winter and its delicate light green in spring.

Climb straight up the mountain from here to a foothill at 1,002 ft. Thence the climb turns north-east to the top of the mountain (1,389 ft). From here you have a fine view of the Mournes, Carlingford Lough, the Cooley Mountains and, to the south and west, Slieve Gullion and the fairy-like hills that make up the Ring Dyke. These little hills are like an illustration by Thomas Mackenzie for James Stephens's *The Crock of Gold*.

From the top go east-south-east towards the forest and enter it by a ride or fire-break between the blocks of trees. There is a variety of trees: Lodgepole and Scots pine, Sitka and Norway spruce, Noble fir and, at the south side, a lot of Japanese and Hybrid larch.

Follow the rides first south-east, then south-west, and then south-east again until you emerge on to the Tamnaghbane road. Follow this to the west and then north along and above the Camlough lake to the starting-point, giving a road walk of 1¾ miles.

Distance: 4 miles.   Ascent: 1,000 ft.   Walking Time: 2 hours.

17. SLIEVE GULLION
This massive hill is very beautiful, lying as it does within the Ring of Gullion — a magnificent Ring Dyke — and surrounded on all sides by the white-washed cottages of small holdings. It is grey and blue and russet brown, and now with more forestry dark

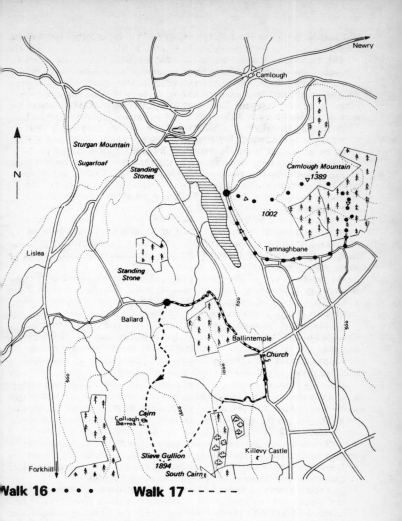

Walk 16 • • •   Walk 17 - - - - -

green, and in the evening when the lights come on in the cottages it has an air of quiet brooding mystery.

Like Slievenamon in Tipperary it is a storied mountain; it is very much part of the folk memory of South Armagh.

The name means the Mountain of Culan, the Smith – the Vulcan of the Gael – who had his fort on or near the mountain. The boy Setanta killed the hound that guarded Culan's fort and in retribution he promised that he would be the hound of Culan and so he became known as Cuchulain.

The mountain is also associated with the later Fianna and Finn McCool. Finn, hunting with his band, startled a white fawn which led him in pursuit all the way to the summit of the mountain. The Fianna were out-distanced in the chase and when they reached the summit Finn was not to be found. They questioned an old, bent, white-haired man sitting by the edge of the lake on the top and found that he was Finn. He had found no white fawn but a beautiful woman who was mourning over the loss of her ring in the waters of the lake. Finn had dived in to recover it and immediately his body shrank into old age. The Fianna thereupon dug the witch who had worked the spell, the Calliagh Bhirra, out of the cairn in which she had hidden and compelled her to remove the charm. Hence the chamber on the top of the mountain is called the Calliagh Bhirra's House and the lake the Calliagh Bhirra's Lake.

You can climb Slieve Gullion from any side, but the way I suggest is from north to south to get the benefit of the long ridge. Park your car at J 025 230 on the mountainy road that runs west to east from a junction one mile south of Lislea. There is a clear and easy track up the south side of the mountain.

At the north end of the summit ridge (1,800 ft) is a round cairn of Bronze Age type, about 50 ft in diameter and 5 ft high, excavated in 1961. Two small cist graves were enclosed by the cairn. Just south of this is the Calliagh Bhirra's Lake.

At the top of the ridge, that is the higher south end (1,894 ft), is the Calliagh Bhirra's House, a cairn nearly 100 ft in diameter and 15 ft high, probably Neolithic in date. It encloses a passage-grave with a passage 15 ft long leading from the south-west side of the cairn to an octagonal burial-chamber, dry-walled and with a corbelled roof.

There is a pleasant by-road running north and south along the east side of the mountain which will bring you back to your car. Drop down north-east towards this, using one of the lanes marked on the 1" map. At J 041 221 on the west side of this road, one mile north of the modern house called Killeavy Castle, are the interesting ruins of Killeavy Church, really two churches joined together. The west church (ninth or tenth century) has a massively lintelled west door, dressed in granite, and a small round-headed east window. The east church may be of thirteenth-century date and has fifteenth-century features.

Distance: 5½ miles.   Ascent: 1,430 ft.   Walking Time: 3 hours.

18. THE HOLYWOOD TO BANGOR COASTAL PATH   A walk on a stretch of low coastline may seem out of place in a book that is largely for hill walkers, but this coast is notable for making a very pleasant walk readily available for the half-million people who live in the Belfast area.

The path to Bangor was the creation of the Ulster Countryside Committee, in association with the Ministry of Development and the District Councils, and is a considerable achievement in land acquisition,

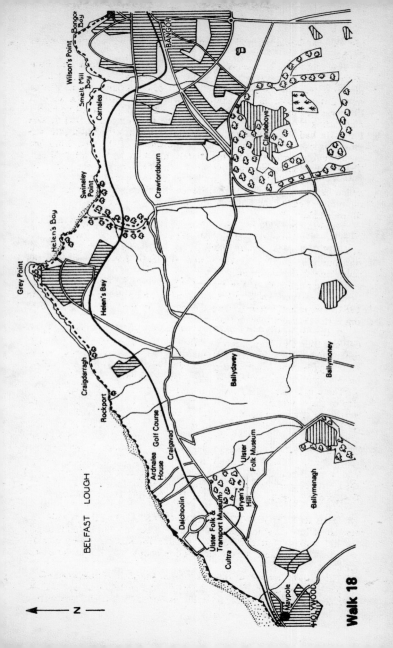

Walk 18

clearing of obstacles, massive reconstruction to deal with erosion by the sea, and regeneration.

Near the junction of High Street and Bangor Road in Holywood are the remains of a small church which marks the site of a Franciscan friary established in the thirteenth century. St. Laisren had founded a monastery in the seventh century and one of the old names for the town is Sanctus Boscus, the holy wood. Not far from the friary church is the Norman motte in Brook Street. John de Courcey founded a town here in the late twelfth century and King John marched through it early in the thirteenth century.

In High Street is Johnnie the Jig, the bronze figure of a small boy playing an accordion. It is by Rosamond Praeger (1867–1954) who has left a number of delightful sculptures and drawings of children and verses about them; she and her brother, Robert Lloyd Praeger, the great naturalist who died in 1953, were natives of Holywood.

Across the street is the Maypole, the only permanent maypole in Ireland. In a drawing of the town made in 1625 a maypole is indicated at the present site.

From the Maypole go down Shore Street, cross the main Bangor road and follow the path. Presently you pass the Cultra Yacht Club and on the right the lower grounds of the very attractive Ulster Folk and Transport Museum, which would need a separate visit. In the grounds there are re-erected buildings, complete with furnishings, which reflect aspects of the social history of Ulster. These exhibits include an eigh-teenth-century cottage, a hip-roofed thatched cottage from Fermanagh, a Coalisland spade mill driven by water power, a Cushendall hill farm cottage and another from Magilligan, a weaver's shop and a mid-nine-teenth-century national school from Ballycastle.

At Craigavad the path goes round the Royal Belfast Golf course where a ramp had to be constructed out to sea to avoid the fairway.

At Rockport the path passes below the well-known Preparatory school of that name. The wooded estate of Craigdarragh contains an old people's home. From here on the wooded lands of the Clandeboye estate, laid out by the Dufferin family, are evident and here a very beautiful two-mile stretch of shore, woodland and glen has been preserved and rehabilitated.

The path goes round Grey Point, which contains gun emplacements from the two World Wars, amid low woods of alder and birch and copses of Scots pine. Walking round Grey Point there is a sense of peace that is quite extraordinary within a few miles of the Belfast conurbation. This quietness is created partly by the way Grey Point reaches out into the Lough and partly by the screen of low trees.

Follow round the Point into Helen's Bay, named after Helen Lady Dufferin. There is a three-mile overgrown avenue, created in 1865, from the beach and the railway station all the way to Clandeboye House; it is interrupted by two roads, but is responsible for some of the belts of trees that make this landscape so attractive. The station buildings are in the Scottish baronial style, with moulded arches, crow-step gables and pointed, lancet windows. They were built for Lord Dufferin to designs by Benjamin Ferrey in the 1860s.

Walk round Helen's Bay towards the boat-house and another wooded point that separates Helen's Bay from Crawfordsburn Bay. As you get round the point, you have a view of Swinely Point, Wilson's Point, Luke's Point and Ballymacormick Point. Walk up the Crawfordsburn Glen through the woods and under a massively beautiful railway bridge which still carries the Holywood-Bangor line opened in 1865. The village of Crawfordsburn is at the head of the glen and if you have the time and money you may eat in the Inn which dates from 1614. Go down the glen on the right bank of Crawford's Burn, a little stream which flows sweetly enough to support kingfishers.

Round another wooded point you come to the tiny Swinely Bay with its coarse sand of broken shells and its amphitheatre of scrub. The path climbs slightly to Swinely Point and continues to Carnalea. It then enters Smelt Mill Bay and goes out round Wilson's Point, finally coming on to the Marine Gardens at Bangor. This bright town is very well equipped with shops, restaurants, swimming-pools and parks. It has an ancient history going back to the foundation of a monastery by St Comgall on a site now occupied by the C. of I. Bangor Abbey church.
Distance: 10 miles.   Ascent: 300 ft.   Walking Time: 3¾ hours.

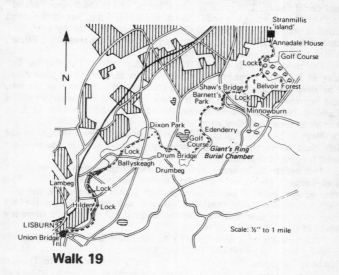

Walk 19

19. THE LAGAN TOWPATH   Union Bridge (1880) in Lisburn is a good place from which to start the walk along the canal, though you could start at the Hillsborough Road Bridge a mile upstream or, if you want a shorter section, at any of the bridges downstream. The Lagan Valley Regional Park stretches from Sprucefield to Stranmillis and, broadly speaking, consists of the landscape which one can see from river and canal.

The Irish linen industry was started in Lisburn in 1698 by Louis Crommelin, a leader of the Huguenots who fled from France in Louis XIV's reign. He is buried in the churchyard of the C. of I. Lisburn cathedral whose spire, as you stand on Union Bridge, rises above the trees of Castle Gardens. The town, including cathedral and castle, was destroyed by an accidental fire in 1707. The cathedral was rebuilt (1708–28) and the beautiful tall and slim octagonal spire was added by David McBlain in 1804–7. In the cathedral there are excellent monuments, including those to William Dobbs who was killed in a naval engagement with Paul Jones off Carrickfergus in 1778; General John Nicholson, the hero of Delhi in 1857; and Bishop Jeremy Taylor who died here in 1667.

Sir Richard Wallace, whose collection of paintings formed the Wallace Collection in London, was Member of Parliament for Lisburn, 1873–85. Both Wallace Park and Castle Gardens in the town have "Wallace" drinking fountains (1872) with their Greek priestesses supporting a dome, like those which he presented to Paris and other cities.

To reach the canal from Union Bridge walk along Hancock Street and Canal Street. The canal is here filled in, and in the former "island" to the left is an unsightly collection of industrial scrap, but the Borough Council proposes to acquire the land and create an amenity area. You pass under a new footbridge, popularly known as the Huguenot Bridge, which neatly conceals a sewage pipe.

The next bridge is that of Hilden, a linen village. The thriving factory of Barbour Threads shows that the fibre industry is far from dead. The river and canal pursue separate courses, with the river to the left, and beyond it the grounds of Glenmore House, the Headquarters of the Lambeg Industrial Development Association, and the belt of trees known as Deadwall Plantation.

Next is Lambeg Bridge with Lambeg, another linen village, on the left. Just below the bridge the brightly coloured poles in the river are used for slalom canoeing.

Just before Ballyskeagh Bridge there is a high mound on which is a lock-keeper's house, now privately owned but becoming derelict. This fine bridge, built of sandstone, has high arches under which the towpath continues. After passing a disused lock you come to the M1 motorway and pass under it. On the wooded hill on the left there is a blaze of rhododendrons in June.

The remains of a lock-keeper's house can still be seen on the left across a little stone bridge. The canal here is almost overgrown, but the landscape is open. On the left are the green slopes of the Sir Thomas and Lady Dixon Park and ahead on the right is the pretty village of Drumbeg with St Patrick's church and its lichgate. On the left of the canal is a well-preserved lock-keeper's house.

Cross over the road at Drum Bridge which carries the Upper Malone Road. Barge-horses here had to cross the road and the remains of the pulleys over which the tow-ropes ran can still be seen on the bridge parapets.

The section from Drum Bridge to Shaw's Bridge is very attractive. Trees line the river banks which in June are white with cow-parsley and in July to September full of the tall pink-purple Himalayan Balsam. Waterhens marshal their young and willow warblers sing sweetly nearby.

There is a long stretch where the river and canal are one. The land is good and actively farmed at New Grove on the right. On the left is the Malone Golf Course at Ballydrain. Edenderry village is passed on the right and near is the Giant's Ring. The National Trust's lands at Terrace Hill and the Minnow Burn lie above and around that small tributary of the Lagan with its beeches and its leafy glades. On the left are the rich sloping meadows of the Barnett Demesne.

Shaw's Bridge (1709), much loved by the people of South Belfast, still stands as a pedestrian bridge, with a new and elegant bridge a short distance downstream, carrying the heavy motor traffic. The towpath goes under the latter. At Shaw's Bridge the path crosses to the right bank. On your right are the Stranmillis College Sports Grounds and on the left is the Newforge factory with its extensive landscaped grounds which now form the Clement Wilson Park. Canoeing is practised on the stretch of water below Shaw's Bridge and there are occasional races from Lisburn to Stranmillis.

You now enter a delightfully secluded stretch of river with the trees of Belvoir Park overhanging on the right and on the left a steep wooded bank.

The canal now cuts off another bend in the river and the resulting "island" is known as "Moreland's Meadow". Steeply rising to the right is the Belvoir Park Forest which contains an educational nature reserve, managed by the Royal Society for the Protection of Birds. The woods continue on the right on Bowling Green Hill.

And so on into Stranmillis which is the end of the Regional Park and the end of this walk. The stretch from Drum Bridge to Stranmillis is particularly rich in bird life. Apart from waterhens and mute swans and the usual woodland birds there are many others to see and hear, especially if you come back and explore the side streams and marshy areas: the kingfisher darting up the Minnowburn; the dipper bobbing and dipping from stone to stone; the grey wagtail flirting at the bridges and the weirs; the sedge warbler in the Deramore marsh; the white-throat at Belvoir and Edenderry; the blackcap occasionally; and the reed bunting in the marsh area of Newforge. The kestrel and sparrow-hawk can also be seen and, more rarely, the long eared owl and barn owl.

Distance: 9¼ miles.   Ascent: nil.   Walking Time: 3 hours.

20. SHANE'S HILL TO GLENARM

If you stay the night in Larne, take the Belfast bus to the point marked on the map (D 368 005) in the area of Kilwaughter. (The service from Kilwaughter past Shane's Hill to Ballymena is infrequent.) You will not have much time for antiquities, but you should know that Kilwaughter Castle (1807) was one of the houses that John Nash built in Ulster in the Gothic style which he was then making fashionable. In Demesne Townland, 300

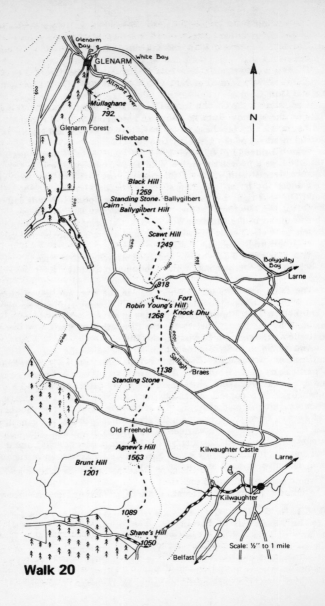

Walk 20

Scale: ½" to 1 mile

44

yards north-north-east of the Castle in a clump of trees, are the remains of an Anglo-Norman motte, possibly built by the Agnew family (Anglo-Norman, D'Agneux) which settled here and gave their name to Agnew's Hill.

You will have a 3½ mile road walk past the foot (855 ft) of Shane's Hill (1,050 ft). Take the path which climbs up the back of Shane's Hill to 1,089 ft.

You are now on the Antrim moors with very little rise and fall until you go down to Glenarm, and with about ten miles of mountain walking, north almost all the way. The first two miles to the top of Agnew's Hill is very gradual. There are fine crags of basalt on the east and north-east side of the hill, and you will hear the pruck of the raven as it wings in and out of the cliffs. From the top the view northwards, even to one who knows Antrim well, is most delightful; layer after layer of undulating moor is laid out from west to east, culminating in a series of escarpments above the blue sea, with a vista of Kintyre, Arran, Sanda and Ailsa Craig and, to the east, Merrick and the Lowther Hills in the Borders of Scotland.

After the gentle decline of Agnew's Hill you cross the road and go north-north-east for the Standing Stone at 1,180 ft. Cross a minor road here and continue for the Sallagh Braes which, if you are botanically inclined, you may wish to explore; but otherwise keep to the top and go over Robin Young's Hill (1,268 ft). Another interesting diversion is the sharp escarpment of Knockdhu, half a mile to the east, where there is a promontory fort. Cross another east-west road at 818 ft and continue (now nearer to the sea) along the top of Scawt Hill (1,249 ft) and Ballygilbert Hill with its cairn and Standing Stone. Go over Black Hill (1,259 ft) and then drop down gradually north-west to a road which will bring you, skirting the forest, into Glenarm.

Distance: 15½ miles.   Ascent: 2,000 ft.   Walking Time: 6½ hours.

21. SALLAGH BRAES TO BLACK HILL FROM BALLYGALLY Y.H.

From the back of the hostel take the field path to the road running to the Old Mill. Follow minor roads as far as Dromain (413 ft). From Killyglen swing round the Sallagh Braes ridge. Explore the Sallagh Braes and Knockdhu, if you wish, but get back on the ridge to the top of Robin Young's Hill and go north over Scawt Hill and Black Hill. Note the steep escarpment of Sugarloaf Hill and drop down to the Moat. Return south by the Old Glenarm Road as far as Carncastle and from there turn east down to the coast.

Distance: 16½ miles.   Ascent: 1,900 ft.   Walking Time: 6¾ hours.

22. THE GARRON PLATEAU

This is a wilderness, a great flat land 1,000–1,200 ft high – a treeless, roadless, and houseless area, tenanted mainly by breeding birds – curlew, redshank, golden plover and colonies of lesser black-backed and blackheaded gulls. Heather, coarse grasses and sedges are abundant and there are many small lakes and pools. The whole place is of great ecological importance and has been noted on a

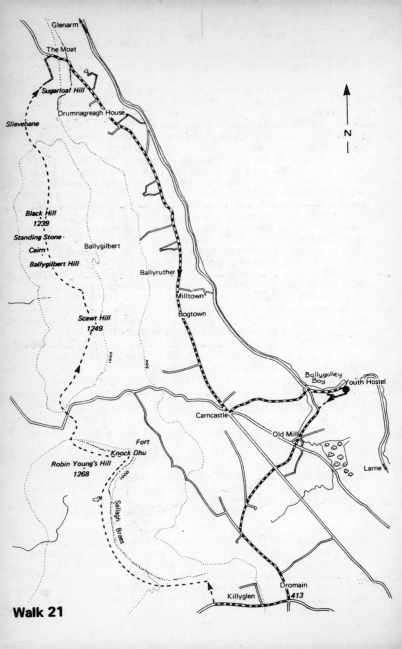

Glenarm

The Moat

Sugarloaf Hill

Drumnagreagh House

Slievebane

Black Hill 1239

Standing Stone

Cairn

Ballygilbert Hill

Ballygilbert

Ballyruther

Milltown

Bogtown

Scawt Hill 1249

Ballygalley Bay

Youth Hostel

Carncastle

Old Mill

Larne

Fort

Knock Dhu

Robin Young's Hill 1268

Sallagh Braes

Dromain
413

Killyglen

N

Walk 21

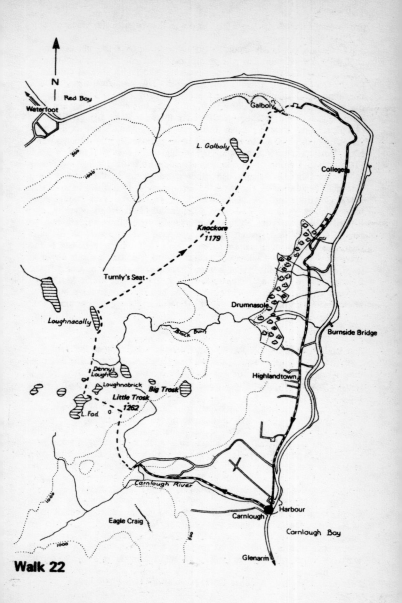

Red Bay

Waterfoot

N

L. Galboly

Galboly

Collegeg

Knockore
1179

Turnly's Seat

Loughnacally

Drumnasole

Block Burn

Burnside Bridge

Denny's
Lough

Loughnabrick

Big Trosk

Highlandtown

Little Trosk
1262

L. Fad

Carnlough River

Eagle Craig

Carnlough

Harbour

Carnlough Bay

Glenarm

Walk 22

47

provisional United Kingdom list for possible recognition internationally as a Biosphere Reserve.

There are obviously many ways of walking over the plateau and I shall give one of them, on the assumption that you are staying in Carnlough. From the village take the road on the north side of the Carnlough River past the former youth hostel. Continue up the glen on the north side and then climb more steeply north-west until you are on the plateau. There are no striking tops to climb, but such as they are they have a directional interest, particularly in mist. Make for Little Trosk (1,262 ft) and then west for the large Lough Fad. There is a whole series of loughs here. Go due north to Loughnacally, the old woman's lake. You have now a walk of 0.7 miles north-east to Turnly's Seat. (Turnly is the name of the local landlords who built the Curfew Tower in Cushendall (1809) and did other good works in the area, with a Georgian residence at the wooded Drumnasole, two miles east of this seat). Continue north-east to Knockore (1,179 ft). You should now have a good vista of Red Bay, Cushendall, Torr Head, Rathlin, the Scottish Isles and the Mull of Kintyre. Continue north-north-east to Lough Galboly and from there drop down to an opening in the cliff face and a delightful winding sheep track. Immediately below is the tiny, almost deserted village of Galboly, and your track winds down to it. Make your way through the village. Keep away from the Coast Road by means of a by-road that runs above it to the back of St MacNissi's College. Continue south by the minor road all the way to Carnlough.
Distance: 14½ miles. Ascent: 1,400 ft. Walking Time: 5¾ hours.

23. LURIGETHAN FROM MONEYVART Y.H.

Cross the bridge in Cushendall and take the second road to the right, a minor one but running straight south-west for 1½ miles. Leave the road and turn left up the north-west slope of the mountain and follow a zig-zag path to the top (1,154 ft).

The top is the end of a basalt spur and contains what Evans considers the finest of several similar promontory forts in Antrim; others are at Knockdhu (see Walk No. 20), Ballygally Head and Cave Hill. There are four ramparts – in places six – with intervening ditches running in a curving line following the contours for a quarter of a mile, ending in steep slopes on the north-west and south-east. Towards the south-east end is an entrance five yards wide, lined with standing stones. Evans dates the fort as probably of the Early Iron Age.

You will now have a very pleasant two-mile walk along the ridge to Crockalough (1,304 ft). From here drop down north to the dull ruins of Retreat Castle. This house was once the terminus of the little narrow-gauge railway from Ballymena and it died of solitude. You now have a pleasant four mile walk back to Moneyvart, with fine views to the north across the bare Glenballyemon. At Ballyfad take the left fork as shown on the map.
Distance: 10 miles. Ascent: 1,400 ft. Walking Time: 4¼ hours.

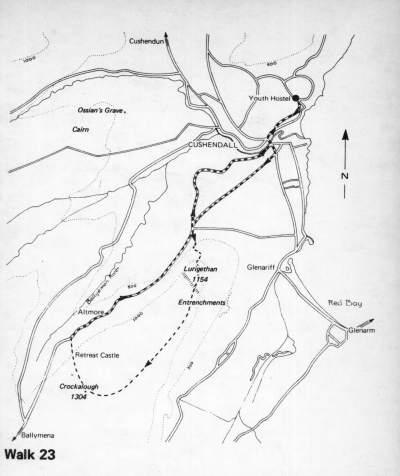

Walk 23

24. TROSTAN AND TIEVEBULLIAGH FROM MONEYVART Y.H.

Walk by the by-road round Glenville and then keep the little hillock
Tieveragh, where the fairies live, on your right. Cross the Cushendun
road and then take the road up Glen Ballyemon, a beautiful but bare
glen flanked by sheep-grazing fields. Follow this towards the Parkmore
Forest. A short distance before the road junction near the top of the
glen there is an old road to the right. Follow this for about half a mile
and then strike north-west across the boggy land for Trostan. The top
(1,817 ft) is a mile away.

From Trostan continue north-north-east to Tievebulliagh, a long

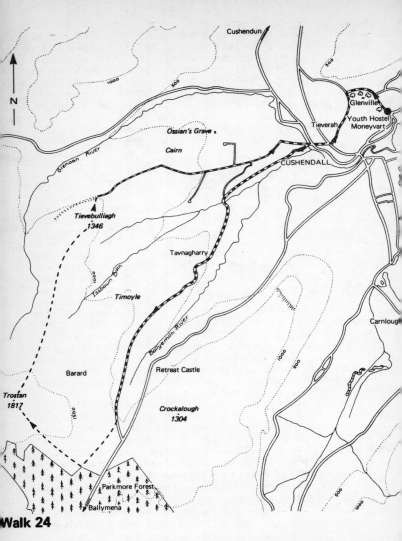

Walk 24

walk across the heather and sedge, with the occasional haunting cry of a curlew, the plaintive 'kee-wi' of a lapwing or the short 'kwup' of a black-headed gull.

Tievebulliagh is another remarkable promontory, much more pointed than Lurigethan. Evans found here a Neolithic axe factory, the most famous in Ireland. Its products have been recognised as far away as Limerick, the Thames Basin and north-east Scotland. A small exposure of bluestone — a metamorphosed interbasaltic rock known as porcellanite — occurs on the east face of the mountain beneath the dolerite sill of the top. The scree below contains 'factory rejects', and on the hilltop (crowned by a Bronze-Age cairn) waste material can be picked up in hollows in the peat. Evans dated the factory to the third millennium B.C.

Drop down to the track which will bring you the whole way (2½ miles) down to where you first crossed the Cushendun road. Cross the road and return to the hostel.

Distance: 12½ miles.   Ascent: 2,000 ft.   Walking Time: 5½ hours.

25. SLIEVEANORRA AND GLENDUN   The idea of this walk is to take you from the comparatively low land that makes up much of Antrim up on to the moors and down to the sea through a very lovely glen. The area of starting is not a tourist one but it should be possible to find farm or country house accommodation in the Kilraughts or Loughguile area. Take an early bus to Loughguile (D 083 254). From this point take the minor road branching north-east to Crockan. Cross the Bush River. Turn east up a little road beside the Aldorough Burn. Continue east-south-east up Slieveanorra to Hugh McPhelim O'Neill's Tomb and the nearby Hugh McPhelim O'Neill's Servant's Tomb. These sites, traditionally associated with a sixteenth-century battle, are barely distinguishable among the heather and peat. They appear to have been two small cairns. The summit of Slieveanorra is a quarter of a mile to the south. Follow the road which runs down north-east from the top to the Cushendall-Armoy road; cross this and take the track through the Beaghs Forest. This follows the Owennaglush River to the Glendun road and river. You are now at the top of Glendun and have before you a long and very pleasant walk down the glen, under the viaduct and into Cushendun, a village which belongs to the National Trust.

Glendun is one of the loveliest of the glens and there are hill farms throughout its length. The road follows the Glendun River all the way. Go under the fine viaduct which carries the main Ballycastle road; it was built by Charles Lanyon in 1839. The Craigagh Wood on your left is covenanted to the National Trust; its great beauty depends on its apparently haphazard mixture of deciduous and pine trees and the way it clothes a rocky hillside with a great variety of effect at different seasons. A few yards inside there is a fine souterrain and at its eastern end in Innispollan, near a cottage, is the 'Altar in the Woods' which has a dimly inscribed cross on a crude altar; this was a Mass Rock used by Roman Catholics until their own church was built a short distance down the road.

There are many interesting houses around the bay: the Georgian Rockport, home of the poet, Moira O'Neill; the Italianate Glenmona, built by Lord Cushendun (Ronald MacNeill) to the design of Clough Williams-Ellis; and the Maud Cottages designed by Clough Williams-Ellis

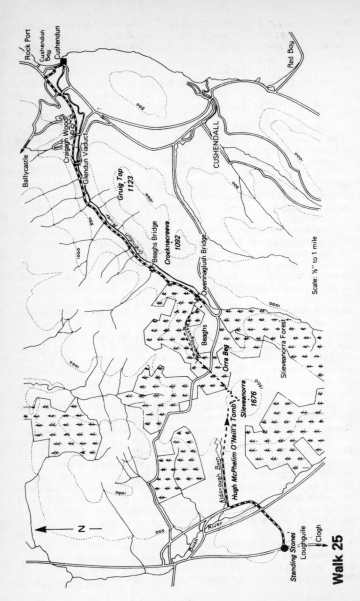

Rock Port
Cushendun Bay
Cushendun

Ballycastle

Craigagh Wood

Glendun Viaduct

Gruig Top
1123

Beaghs Bridge

Crocknacreeva
1092

CUSHENDALL

Red Bay

Owennaglush Bridge

Beaghs

Orra Beg

Slieveanorra Forest

Slieveanorra
1676

Hugh McPhelim O'Neill's Tomb

Idorough Burn

Bush River

Standing Stones

Loughguile

Clogh

N

Scale: ½" to 1 mile

Walk 25

52

in a Cornish style to commemorate Lord Cushendun's wife Maud who was born in Penzance. See also Walks 26, 27 and 28.

Distance: 14½ miles.   Ascent: 1,200 ft.   Walking Time: 5½ hours.

26. CUSHENDUN FROM MONEYVART Y.H.

26. CUSHENDUN FROM MONEYVART Y.H. The by-roads of Cushendall and Cushendun are so pleasant that they repay exploration.

Leave Moneyvart by the coast road and go north to the Church ruins at Layde, a place of peaceful beauty. Part of the ruins are perhaps of the thirteenth century, part later. There is a stone dated 1696 in a round-arched doorway in the south wall which may be the date of an addition to the east end; this stone was probably put there for its preservation.

From the church there is a path down to the shore, but walking along the shore is difficult. Go back to the road and continue north towards Cushendun with good views of the bay. The road drops down to the village of Knocknacarry. Continue to the right of Cushendun. Note the salmon fishery and round the point see the winding tunnel at the entrance to the Caves House. There is a series of caves in this mass of conglomerate rock or 'pudding-stones' in the old red sandstone; they are on a 'raised beach' where the sea level was at one time many feet higher than it is to-day. The house, now occupied by a religious order, was built in 1820 by de la Cherois Crommelin (but considerably rebuilt in 1850) and was the home of John Masefield's wife, a member of the Crommelin family.

Walk across the bridge and along the whin-fringed green or the golden sands. At the other end of the shore is the estuary of the Brablagh Burn which you can cross by stepping-stones. See Rockport (c. 1815) in its very beautiful setting, the home of the poetess, Moira O'Neill (Nesta Higginson). Walk through the tiny hamlet of Milltown and go round the west side of the square-towered slim-pinnacled C. of I. Church (c. 1838) among the trees. Its interior is simple and austere. Continue round the church and through the village. Walk back by Knocknacarry. Continue south-west and return by the middle road. At Ballybrack take a lane to the left which will bring you back to the hostel.

Distance: 8½ miles.   Ascent: 1,000 ft.   Walking Time: 3½ hours.

27. GLENAAN AND GLENDUN FROM MONEYVART Y.H.

27. GLENAAN AND GLENDUN FROM MONEYVART Y.H. From the hostel go round the north side of Glenville and get to the Glenaan road (168 ft) by any of the ways which can be seen on the 1" map. A little over half a mile along this road there is a lane on the left leading to Ossian's Grave. This megalithic tomb stands in a field at 450 ft. It is a segmented gallery-grave or 'horned cairn'. The burial gallery, divided into two chambers, opens on to a semi-circular forecourt bounded by two 'horns' of upright stones. It is of Neolithic date (2500 to 2000 B.C.) and is therefore older than Ossian, a warrior and poet of early Christian times.

Continue up Glenaan, following the road which rises to 958 ft before dropping to the Glendun River. Take the road to the right down

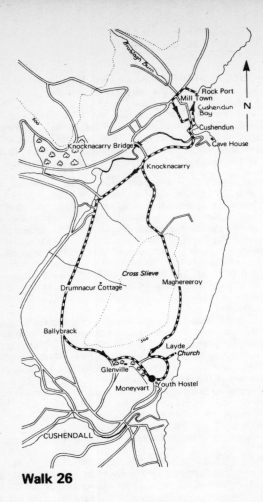

Walk 26

Glendun, with Beaghs Forest on your left. In 1963 there was a landslide on the north side of the river and road which did great damage by unleashing a flood down the river. There are four fords by which the two or three farmers who remain on the right bank can get vehicles and animals across, and there are three footbridges. You may use any of the footbridges to explore the right bank, but there is no continuous path on that side. Subject to permission from the farmer, however, you may, by crossing the third footbridge (at D 203 318), continue your walk

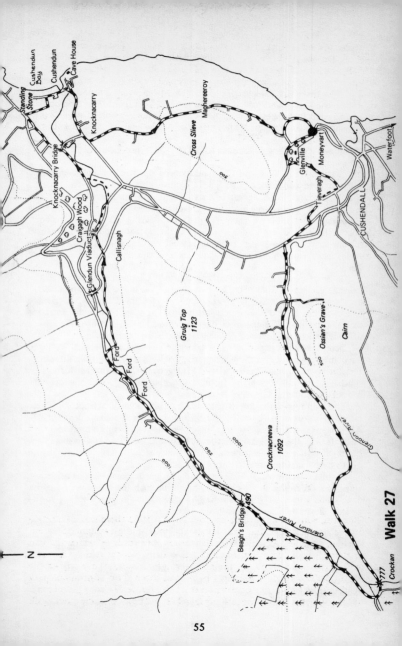

N

Cushendun Bay
Cushendun
Cave House
Standing Stone
Knocknacarry
Maghereeroy
Cross Slieve
Waterfoot
Glenville
Moneyvart
Tieveragh
CUSHENDALL
Knocknacarry Bridge
Craigagh Wood
Glendun Viaduct
Callisnagh
Ossian's Grave
Cairn
Gruig Top
1123
Crocknacreeva
1092
Ford
Ford
Ford
Glendun River
Glencloon River
Beagh's Bridge
490
Crockan
777

Walk 27

55

above the right bank right down to Clady Bridge. Take care to close all gates. Do not go down to the viaduct which carries the main Cushendall/Ballycastle road; keep above this road and you will cross it at D 222 320. Keep on down to Clady Bridge. Don't cross this, but take a path near it down to the right bank of the river. This path will take you along the meandering river and will bring you over it by a footbridge and out on to the road just below the Roman Catholic church. And so on down to Cushendun. Return to Moneyvart via Knocknacarry and the Layde coast road.

Distance: 16¼ miles.   Ascent: 1,250 ft.   Walking Time: 6½ hours.

28. TORR HEAD   From Cushendun take the 'corkscrew' road. Take a by-road to the left at D 235 330. Follow this road till you come to the 'corkscrew' road again; cross this and continue straight over the moors along a green road. After two miles you will see, at a distance of a quarter of a mile on the left, the disappearing lake, Loughaveema. Porous limestone lies under the mud at the bottom, and when the level of the surrounding water table drops below that in the lake, the lake water drains out quickly and finds its way underground to the Carey River.

Go north over the long heathery moor of Carnanmore and reach the cairn at the top at 1,253 ft. The passage-grave is one of a group in north-east Antrim. The cairn is 15 ft high and 75 ft in diameter. A passage 4 ft wide can be traced running south-west for 10½ ft from the entrance to the chamber. The chamber has a corbelled roof, some of the stones of which show much worn concentric circles and cup-marks.

Drop down to the north and take the road to Torr Head. You will have interesting scrambling along the rocky shore in either direction. Return to the coastal road at the bridge over the Altmore Burn. This road is very quiet, but the farmers are glad to talk and the primary school overlooking Loughan Bay is busy.

The winding walk down into Cushendun is very attractive. Three hundred yards north-west of the bridge over the Tornamoney Burn in Altagore is a cashel. A 10 ft thick dry-stone wall forms a circle 50 ft in diameter. In the thickness of the wall on the west side is a passage now blocked with stones. The cashel is like some sites in Argyle settled from north-east Antrim in the fifth century A.D.

A mile north-west of Milltown and 200 yards north-east of Milltown Burn is a collapsed single-chamber megalith with the remains of a cairn. 600 yards north of this, at a height of 700 ft, there is another round cairn containing a small megalithic chamber.

As you come towards Rockport House there are the ivied remains of Castle Carra. It was here that Shane O'Neill came to try to form an alliance with Sorley Boy MacDonnell in 1567, when a banquet was staged in his honour, at the end of which he was murdered.

In a field on your left are two fine standing stones, 6 ft high. Salmon are netted at the mouth of the Dun River and upstream trout, sea trout and salmon are angled for.

Distance: 16½ miles.   Ascent: 2,250 ft.   Walking Time: 7 hours.

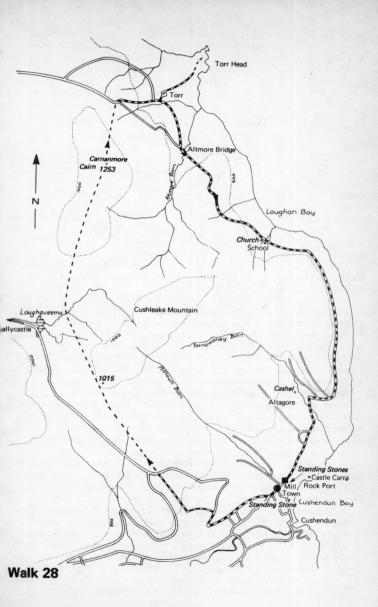

Torr Head

Torr

Altmore Bridge

Altmore Burn

Loughan Bay

Carnanmore
Cairn 1253

N

Church
School

Loughaveema

allycastle

Cushleake Mountain

Tornamoney Burn

1015

Tillawn Burn

Cashel
Altagore

Standing Stones
• Castle Carra
Rock Port

Mill
Town

Standing Stone Cushendun Bay

Cushendun

Walk 28

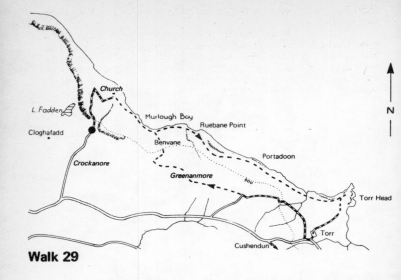

Walk 29

29. MURLOUGH BAY   This is a special place, much loved by naturalists and walkers, and fortunately now protected by the National Trust. There are two hill farms in the enclosing area, one of them, Benvane, now in Trust hands. Grazing rights are still held by the farmers.

The bay contains a great variety of rocks. To the north is Fair Head, with its gigantic columns resting on carboniferous sandstone, shale and beds of coal. In the centre there are high cliffs of white chalk, overlying bright red Triassic sandstone. The southern horn of the bay is made up of ancient mica-schists, an outlying fragment of the rocks of Donegal. The wet surface of the red sandstone is the home of the yellow saxifrage *(Saxifraga aizoides)*, showing up well in July and August down to the level of the sea. In spring there are primroses and wild hyacinths, red campion and ferns.

There is a small lake, Lough Faddan, to the west of the road down to the bay. On a rocky knoll 525 yards south-west of the lake is a mutilated horned cairn, almost hidden in heather. There appear to have been three chambers totalling 27 ft in length and opening to the north-east.

Leave your car at the Trust car park above the bay near the Casement memorial. Walk down by the winding track on the west side. There is a very small church at Drumnalis at the western end of the bay, only 33 ft by 18 ft outside, with not more than 30 inches remaining in the height of the walls. Ten feet to the north of the west end is a small cross of crude workmanship.

Walk along the track to the sandy bay. Climb round the rocky Ruebane Point and continue near the shore to Portadoon. Look out for foxes here in the rough vegetation and rocks of the hillside. Keep on to Torr Head.

To return take to the road from Torr Head for two miles until you come to about D 214 406 and then strike north-west across the moor past some converted wartime buildings for Greenanmore. Drop down towards the Benvane farmhouse. Climb down steeply through the mixed woodland to the bay. Return up the track to your car.

Distance: 8 miles.   Ascent: 1,450 ft.   Walking Time: 3½ to 4 hours.

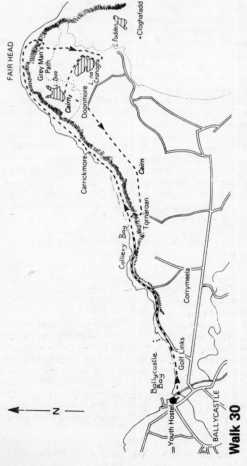

30. FAIR HEAD FROM BALLYCASTLE Y.H.

FAIR HEAD FROM BALLYCASTLE Y.H. Fair Head is one of the great headlands of Ireland. It is magnificent when seen from Ballycastle or from any of the headlands on the north coast. The massive basaltic cliff falls sheer for nearly 600 ft. Its base and face are so inaccessible that a pair of golden eagles was able to nest here and rear two young in 1953. After that their nesting was intermittent and ceased in 1960.

From the hostel walk along the shore of the bay to the east end of the strand and the North Star Dyke and join the little road that runs above the rocks towards Fair Head. Pass the Corrymeela Community Centre, the old coal mine workings, Colliery Bay and Carrickmore, and continue as far as the track will bring you. You now face a very formidable scramble over fallen boulders with overgrown crevices. There is the danger of a sprained ankle, so don't go alone. If any member of the party is not fit for tough scrambling it would be better to climb at once to the moors.

Benmore (the great headland) or Fair Head looks across to Rathlin and to Kintyre. Lower Carboniferous sandstones, lying in horizontal beds, were invaded by a mass of molten lava, which squeezed its way in between the layers, forming a solid bed of basalt (dolerite) about three feet thick. Having solidified slowly between two cold surfaces, it has assumed a columnar structure, at right angles to the planes of cooling, as at the Giant's Causeway, but here the columns are some 50 ft in width and hundreds of feet high. The sandstones which originally formed the cover of the sill have been removed by denudation; only traces of them remain and the wide heathy area on the top of the head is the upper surface of the volcanic intrusion.

Continue round the Head until you see a gap in the cliff, the Grey Man's Path. It is important to find this, as it is the only way of climbing the Head once you have started scrambling round it, unless you go on to Murlough Bay.

Climb up the Grey Man's Path; this is stiff enough, but easier than going down. From the top go down gradually south to Lough na Cranagh and see the crannog, an artificial island or lake-dwelling. It is oval in shape, approximately 120 ft by 90 ft and is faced with a dry-built revetment five to seven ft above the water level.

South-east of the lake there is a mutilated cairn. After seeing it, return north-east past the lake and climb to Lough Doo. Three hundred yards south-west of this dark lough and 50 yards from the sea cliff there is a 'sepulchral mound' as it was called on the old OS maps; it is now called a 'cairn'. It is covered with grass and heather, but the cairn stones are visible in places. It appears to be a round passage-grave cairn, 16 yards in diameter, occupying the sloping top of a 'roche moutonnée' on the glaciated plateau which terminates in Fair Head. The term 'roche moutonnée' was given in 1796 by de Saussure to a glaciated rock hill resembling the fleecy, ruffled, curled wig which was fashionable during the late eighteenth century. Such rocks have rounded surfaces sloping gently in the direction of the ice movement, with the steeper slopes on the lee side, due to the plucking action of the ice.

Continue south to Doonmore. This is a typical motte and bailey fort carved out of a natural outcrop of basalt probably about 1180 by an early Anglo-Norman settler. It is oval in plan and was originally surrounded by stone walls (3 to 4 ft thick) of which little more than the foundations now remain.

Continue south-west across the moors and parallel to the sea for 1 mile and you will come to a cairn circle, marked on the 1" map, 300 yards from the sea. It is 17 yards in diameter and a number of stones of the peristalith survive, set on edge. There are traces of a megalithic chamber, perhaps a passage-grave.

At Tornaroan you can drop down to the coastal path and return by the shore to Ballycastle.

Distance: 11 miles.   Ascent: 800 ft.   Walking Time: 5 hours.

31. KNOCKLAYD

(a) **From Ballycastle Y.H.:** From the hostel go to the Diamond in the upper town where the famous Ould Lammas Fair is held for two days at the end of every August. Note the C.of I. Church (1756) with its lofty octagonal spire, the late Georgian houses and the fluted-columned porch of the Antrim Arms Hotel. Go by Fair Hill and follow the line of the old narrow-guage railway for a few hundred yards. Turn up into the forest at the picnic site. Follow the track up through the forest for about a mile to the car park and strike off to the right, crossing the forest boundary fence by a stile on to the open moor. From here the way to the top is marked by posts, though the slope by the fence on the left side is dryer.

The basalt dome of the hill is crowned by an Ordnance Survey pillar and by Carn-na-Truagh, a cairn 12 ft high, 65 ft in diameter and comparatively unbroken, being protected by peat. It is possible that it may cover a passage-grave like the similarly placed cairn Carnanmore 6½ miles to the east-north-east.

Go west down to the road about half a mile north of Capecastle, and back north to Ballycastle.

Distance: 8½ miles.   Ascent: 1,700 ft.   Walking Time: 4 hours.

(b) **Including Breen:** Follow the same route to the top of Knocklayd as in (a) above. Descend to the south, however, from the top and walk to the junction of the Drumavoley and Glenshesk roads and take a lane to the south. After about 200 yards the lane turns east. On the right is a school outdoor pursuits centre and in the field on the left is a Standing Stone. Continue on into Breen Wood. Forty-five acres of this wood form a National Nature Reserve. Sessile and pedunculate oaks are the dominant species, associated with birch, ash, rowan, holly, hazel and hawthorn, with alder and willow along streams. Follow the path through the forest until it emerges in the valley of the Glenshesk River at Ardagh. It is an easy climb to the spot (D 133 318) where a simple incised stone marks the site of McQuillan's grave. Return north by the track along the river to the Glenshesk road (385 ft). Note the glacial overflow channels. Cross the Glenshesk road by a track to the Drumavoley road and in this way return above the west bank of the river to Ballycastle.

Distance: 14 miles.   Ascent: 2,300 ft.   Walking Time: 6¼ hours.

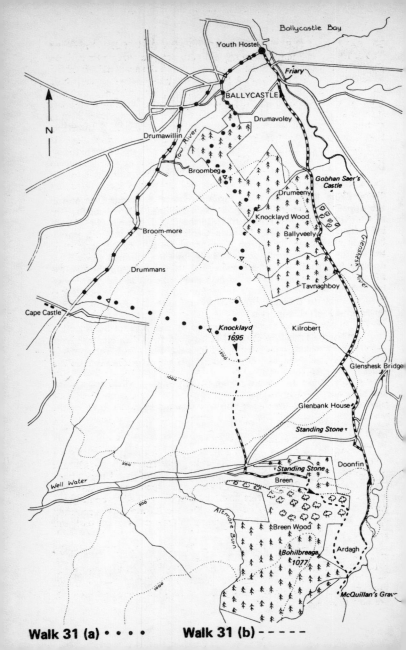

Walk 31 (a) • • •   Walk 31 (b) - - - -

32. BALLYCASTLE Y.H. TO WHITE PARK BAY Y.H.

From the Youth Hostel you may like to try climbing along an overgrown path on the cliff-top towards the coast-guard lookout on the headland. However, to start your walk to White Park Bay you will find it better to keep to the road, which is still uncluttered by traffic, for a short distance until you get past Clare Park. Where the county road turns sharply to the left leave it and go straight on down a lane. Follow this and ask permission to find your way down to the rough rocky shore at Portcarn, Doon and Port Campbell. From here it is a very hard scramble to Portnakillew. (If you have a heavy pack or don't like scrambling, you would be better to stay on the county road up to the point where you can turn down to Kinbane and Portnakillew.) Portnakillew is a small amphitheatre; its sides are steep and rocky with a dense lush growth of trees, ferns and mosses down to the rocky shore where there is a small area of coarse sand. Climb up to the top in zig-zag fashion and reach the by-road which goes out to Kinbane. Note the ice-house on the left near the car park. Drop down the steep path to the tiny port and to Kinbane Castle, which is at the narrow end of a great pear-shaped chalk rock. The castle is defended first by the steepness of the approach — for 25 feet there is a gradient of seven in six. There are the remains of a massive rectangular gate-tower in the centre of a stout wall from cliff edge to cliff edge. The tower was of three stories and measures 33 ft square, with walls 4 ft thick. To the north-east of the outer defence was the bawn, but most of it has disappeared with cliff erosion. It was built by Colla MacDonnell, brother of Sorley Boy, in 1547.

Return by the by-road to the county road and continue west along it for 2¼ miles, until you come to the National Trust's way down to Carrick-a-raide. Here there is a fishery situated on a stack, a grass-topped perpendicular island, Carrick-a-raide (the rock in the road — that is, the road of the salmon). There is no sort of harbour anywhere convenient, and the boats have to be hoisted on to the rock by a crane fixed on a platform of rock on the sheltered south-east side, about 20 ft above the water. The fishermen have built a rope-bridge to bring them to the island. Under the rope-bridge is a deep channel where the salmon run across the vent of an extinct volcano.

Follow the path west round a great scythe of limestone cliff for a mile to Larry Bane (*laragh bane,* the white site). This was a magnificent headland of white limestone that appeared in one of Paul Henry's best-known paintings. For the sake of local employment and because of a weakness in planning law, this headland, which had been crowned by a prehistoric fort, was largely cut away. The site has now been acquired by the National Trust which is providing an amenity area, car park and possibly a caravan park.

Half a mile north of Larry Bane is Sheep Island, a perpendicular stack with a flat grassy top. It is a great breeding ground for puffins, razorbills and guillemots, but for some years was infested by rats. However, the British army and marines landed the National Trust wardens by helicopter on the island to lay poison in suitable places and the birds are now breeding in peace.

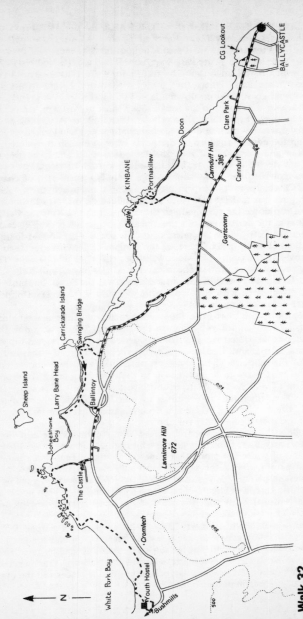

Walk 32

There is no right of way to the west, so you should go back to the road, through Ballintoy village, and down past the Castle farm and the C. of I. church to Ballintoy Harbour. The tower of the church has a distinct batter and small defensive windows and doors; there are large windows with elliptical tops in the body of the church. In the clear northern light this bright white church is unusually attractive. The harbour is vivid with its white piers, white beach and black cliffs and islands.

Having passed through the harbour you are now on a 'raised beach' as you approach the eastern end of the two mile strand of White Park Bay which was acquired by the National Trust in 1939.

White Park Bay is a magnificent natural amphitheatre of limestone, but out at sea, at lower levels, stacks of black rock rise from the water, showing how the surface of the land has cracked and portions have dropped down hundreds of feet as a result of disturbance.

On the top of a small hillock of slipped chalk near the centre of the Bay at D 022 440 is a small circular cairn 36 ft in diameter. Many of the basalt stones, averaging 3 ft in length, have fallen down the slope. Two neolithic sites have been explored: one, just west-south-west of this cairn, at D 021 439; and the other near the eastern end at D 029 447. Quantities of bones (including those of the great auk) charcoal and flint instruments have been found. The great auk was a cousin of the razorbill and guillemot. Like the penguin it had rudimentary wings quite unfit for flying and stood about three feet high. Its bones have also been found in middens in Waterford, Clare and Donegal. The only known Irish specimen is preserved in the Museum at Trinity College, Dublin; it was taken alive in Waterford in 1834 and died in the same year. The species became extinct in 1844.

Climb up to the hostel, nicely sited in the south-west part of the bay. **Distance: 10½ miles.   Ascent: 750—1,500 ft.   Walking Time: 4 hours,** but up to 6½ hours if Doon, Portnakillew, Kinbane and Carrick-a-raide are explored.

33. WHITE PARK BAY TO GIANT'S CAUSEWAY The Giant's Causeway attracted so many visitors in the eighteenth and nineteenth centuries that, like the Lakes of Killarney, it built up a small industry. There was an old woman looking after the wishing-well, and there were jarveys and boatmen, and huts and stalls for souvenirs. There were also gates and an entrance charge was made. In 1962 the National Trust, with a grant from the Northern Ireland government, acquired the land, removed the gates and huts, and admitted the public free of charge.

The Trust then started to obtain access from the farmers along the cliffs. The Ulster farmer loves his land and farms the headlands right to the cliff edge, either with sheep or cattle or in barley. Where the farmer would not sell the strip of coast or cliff, the Trust negotiated an agreement with him and provided fencing and stiles. In this way the Trust has completed a path from Carrick-a-raide to Portballintrae, a distance of about 14 miles.

From the hostel go down to the shore and walk along to Portbrad-

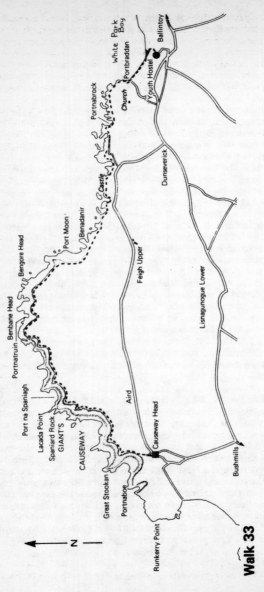

Walk 33

N

Ballintoy
White Park Bay
Portbraddan
Youth Hostel
Church
Portnabrock
Castle
Dunseverick
Port Moon
Benadanir
Bengore Head
Feigh Upper
Benbane Head
Portnatruin
Port na Spaniagh
Lisnangonue Lower
Lacada Point
Spaniard Rock
GIANT'S
CAUSEWAY
Great Stookan
Aird
Portnaboe
Causeway Head
Runkerry Point
Bushmills

66

dan, a very pleasant fishing village. There is a tiny, privately built church on the left, which you may see if you seek permission. It is called St Gobhan's after the patron saint of builders. Three hundred yards to the west are the ruins of Templastragh (*Teampul Lasrach,* the Church of the Flame), chiefly of interest for the ancient incised cross-slab built into the remains of the west gable for preservation. These remains are probably of early sixteenth-century date, but there was a seventh-century church on the site.

Continue round the coast past stacks and tiny inlets: Portacallan, Portachornan, Portnabrock (the badger's port), Portninish, the March Foot, the Sandy Ope to Portnaweelan, the port of Dunseverick village. 'Port' means a landing-place; curraghs and other small craft may have been able to land in these perilous places.

Continue for half a mile to Dunseverick Castle, a ruin held by the National Trust. The pear-shaped rock on which the ruin – probably a sixteenth-century gatehouse – stands was fortified from earliest times. Its name, Dun Sobhairce, is said in the *Annals of the Four Masters* to be derived from the chieftain who first fortified it. One of the five great roads that radiated from Tara terminated here and the name occurs in many of the ancient Irish tales. St Patrick is said in various accounts to have visited it and blessed it. It was stormed by the Danes in 870 and 924. The site was in possession of the O'Cahan family in the sixteenth century (perhaps earlier).

You will then come to Portnahastul, Portnahooagh (Port of the Cave), Benadanir (the Dane's Peak), with its fine hexagonal columns, Stac-na-cuil-dubh and Port Moon. Port Moon and Port Fad, a little further on, are still actively used for salmon fishing. The net used is known as a 'bag' net, a Scottish invention introduced to North Antrim in the 1830s.

The remainder of the walk is entirely delightful and in one sense does not need a guide book. But a study of the place-names will help. The older name of the Giant's Causeway was Clachanafomhaire, the stepping-stones of the Fomorians, the small dark men who inhabited Ireland before the Gaelic-speaking peoples arrived. The Stookins are rock-like stacks of corn or flax, the same Gaelic word being used. Portnacalliagh is the port of the old woman, while Portnatrachen is the port of lamentation – from the moaning sound made by the wind through a fissure in the rock. Bengore is the peak of the goats, and Portmadagh Ruadh is the port of the red dog, that is, the fox.

You will hear the 'pruck' of the raven. You will see the kestrel and sparrow-hawk and you may see high overhead the peregrine falcon. At nesting times you will see razorbills and guillemots on the cliff ledges. There are puffins in burrows and black guillemots tumbling in the sea below, and the ever-present fulmar petrel gliding on the thermal currents.

You will see fine hexagonal basalt columns at Port Fad and Bengore and again when you round Benbane. Here you begin to see the magnificent series of bays and amphitheatres and stacks that make up the Causeway. You are on the top of the 'Middle Basalt' which is the layer that contains the typical hexagonal columns. The Lower Basalts have no columns; the two series, Lower and Middle, are separated by the very distinctive reddish Interbasaltic Bed. It is this bed which the lower cliff path follows (where you should make a later walk). It is the result of the weathering of the top flow of the Lower Basalts, which took place during a period of quiessence in volcanic activity and which lasted perhaps a million years before the first flow of the Middle layers took place. The bed is 30 to 40 ft thick and contains fossil plants.

From the top, after you round Benbane, you will see many dykes. Their dark dolerite rock is very hard and resistant. One can be seen cutting through the basalt above Port na Tober (the Port of the Well) and others are on the foreshore at Port na Spaniagh, Port Reostan, Port Noffer (the Giant's Port) and Portnaboe (the Cow's Port).

In September 1588, the *Gerona*, one of four great galleasses in the Spanish Armada, laden with men and treasure, sank off the Causeway and 264 bodies were washed up in Port na Spaniagh. In 1968 the *Gerona* story was pieced together by the Belgian underwater explorer Robert Stenuit. On an OS map he found 'Spanish Rock', 'Spaniard Cave' and 'Port na Spaniagh'. Since these names had been handed down by generations of fishermen, he searched the seabed below. He eventually found the wreck at Lacada Point (the point of the long flagstone) which you can see lying between Spaniard Cave and Port na Spaniagh. The *Gerona* treasure can now be seen in the Ulster Museum, Belfast.

Continue round Aird Snout and Weir's Snout to Causeway Head. Here there is a National Trust cafe and information centre, where you can obtain an excellent illustrated guide to the Causeway. The Trust operates a mini-bus service for those wishing to travel by road between Causeway Head and Dunseverick Castle. There is hotel and farmhouse accommodation.

Distance: 7½ miles. Ascent: 400 ft. Walking Time: 2½ to 4 hours.

34. GIANT'S CAUSEWAY TO PORTRUSH

At Causeway Head, if you are walking westwards, you have not quite come to the end of this magnificent stretch of cliff scenery. Walk along the path that runs at the back of the hotel, westwards along the cliff-top. (If you are staying here, you should try to get a boat to explore the caves from the Brenther slip which the National Trust has reconstructed at Portnaboe.) Note the two dykes in Portnaboe, one called the Camel's Back near the slip. As you walk round the head, below you is the long narrow Portcoon Cave. You can enter this cave from the land by a side passage on the western side of the head, but care is needed at high tide. The other caves, Pigeon Rock and Runkerry, are only accessible from the sea.

Rock pigeons and ferral pigeons fly in and out of the cliffs. Go in round the long inlet of Leckilroy cove. Off Runkerry Point is a prominent rock, the Mile Stone, and inland from it you are passing just above Runkerry Cave which is over 700 ft long.

There is a salmon fishery off Black Rock. Runkerry House, now a well-kept old people's home, which you pass, was built for Lord Mac-Naghten in 1883.

Walk along Bushfoot Strand or use, for part of the way, the line of

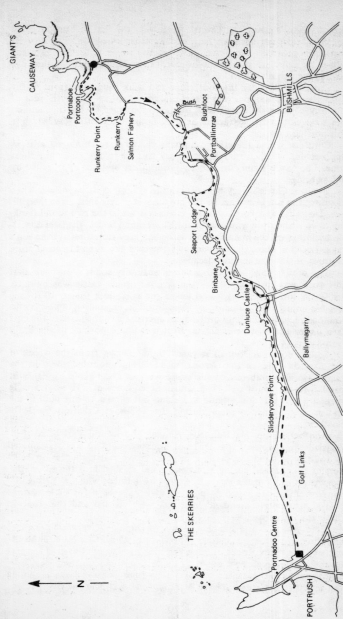

GIANT'S
CAUSEWAY

Portnaboe
Portcoon
Runkerry Point
Runkerry
Salmon Fishery
R. Bush
Bushfoot
Portballintrae
BUSHMILLS
Seaport Lodge
Binbane
Dunluce Castle
Ballymagarry
Slidderycove Point
Golf Links
Portnadoo Centre
THE SKERRIES
PORTRUSH

N

Walk 34

the old Giant's Causeway Electric Tramway, the first in Europe, 1883 to 1950, that ran between here and Portrush. A waterfall up river at Bushmills provided the power. Two of the water mills that gave the village its name are still in good order, as also is Bushmills whiskey distillery, the world's oldest.

Cross the Bush by the footbridge and walk round the front of the attractive little harbour and resort of Portballantrae. On both sides of the tiny bay are shelves of rock that are submerged by the tide, and on the west side is the attractive Seaport Lodge (c. 1770), very white in this northern setting.

Continue round the cliff to Binbane and so on to Dunluce Castle, in approaching which it may be necessary to take to the road for a short time. The castle stands on a rocky promontory and was approached by a drawbridge.

Dunluce Castle is very beautiful in the evening light, especially when at sunset the sun blazes across the northern sea, over Inishowen, Magilligan, Downhill and Portrush. The mediaeval walls, the two round flanking towers, the wide windows of the Elizabethan house, the later domestic buildings on the mainland, all with their grey stones reflect the sun's rays. Looking through the windows towards the sunset, you capture pictures of this sparkling landscape.

The prefix 'dun' is an indication of antiquity and it is probable that this rock was fortified before the Anglo-Norman castle was built (c. 1300). A souterrain was found under the north-east tower, 40 ft long and big enough for a man to squeeze through, expanding in places into rounded recesses; the only outlet is an aperture a foot square in the cliff face under the north-east tower. In it was found pottery of the Early Iron Age (c. 400 B.C.)

Sorley Boy MacDonnell salvaged three cannon from the wreck of the Armada galleass, the *Gerona*, in 1588 and mounted them in the castle. He also embellished his castle with an avant-garde loggia, built parallel to the south wall. The sandstone columns of a five-bay arcade suggest a construction unique in Ireland but similar to one built in the Italian Renaissance manner during the 1580s at Crichton Castle in Scotland.

Another of the MacDonnells, Randal, the second Earl of Antrim, married the widow of that Duke of Buckingham who was assassinated in 1628; she found the castle lonely. To make matters worse, in 1639 part of it collapsed during a reception and crashed into the sea, carrying with it most of the servants, except for a tinker who was sitting in a window-embrasure mending pots. It may have been for these reasons that the extensive mainland buildings were erected and that the old castle fell into disuse.

Here you will find the blue Flower of Dunluce *(Geranium pratense)* and the pale pink Sand Spurrey *(Spergularia rubra)*. Continue round the cliffs to the White Rocks, though you may have to use the road for part of the way. A road goes down to the White Rocks on their west side; you should see these cliffs of chalk with their exciting caves, including the 195 ft long Cathedral Cave, the Elephant Arch and the Giant's Paw.

Go past Slidderycove point and walk into Portrush by the strand or over the sandhills. Out to sea are the Skerries and on the front by Lansdowne Green and near the Blue Pool is the tiniest of Nature Reserves, a group of rocks which played a big part in the history of geology and settled the battle between the Neptunists and the Vulcanists. In the rocks can be seen the spiral patterns of fossil ammonites, sea creatures of 150 million years ago. (For further information call at the nearby Portandoo Countryside Centre, open in the holiday season.)

Distance: 8 miles.   Ascent: 300 ft.   Walking Time: 3½ hours (excluding Dunluce Castle).

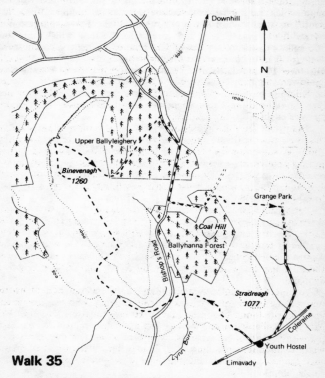

Walk 35

35. BINEVENAGH FROM STRADREAGH Y.H. From the hostel walk north-west up the improved lane that runs at the base of Stradreagh mountain. Cross the Lynn Burn, and strike on to the Bishop's Road. Continue west and then north-west along an old lane past Douglas's farm and along the base of Binevenagh to McIntyre's farm. Climb to the top of the ridge and continue north right along this to the top

71

(1,260 ft). The ridge above the 1000 ft contour stretches for nearly 2¼ miles and offers a continuing panorama of the North Derry fields stretching out to the Magilligan sandhills and strand. Lough Foyle sweeps round from its narrow entry at Magilligan Point and Moville and away south-west to the city of Londonderry. Further to the west are the hills of the Inishowen peninsula. On the summit is a car park and a lake which, although artificially formed, is attractive.

You may explore the top of the ridge and the cliff edge for a further half mile in a northerly direction. Then make south-east for the southern end of the Ballyleighery Forest. From here there is a track going north-east through the forest. Follow this until you reach the road which runs south-east. Follow this to the Bishop's Road. Walk south for 1 mile. Turn left at the road past the TV mast to the north of the Ballyhanna Forest, and go east to the road which runs south through Grange Park townland. This road will bring you to the Murder Hole road, and you turn right for the hostel.

Distance: 10 miles.   Ascent: 1,200 ft approx.   Walking Time: 4 hours.

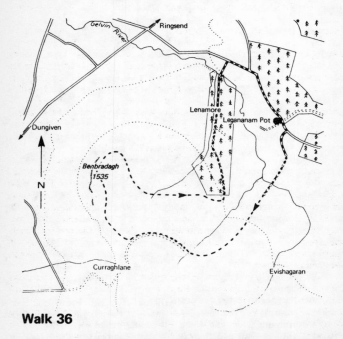

Walk 36

36. BENBRADAGH FROM LEGANANAM POT Benbradagh presents a notable basalt escarpment when seen from Dungiven and the valley of the Roe. Legananam Pot is a suitable place at which to park; it is east-north-east of the summit of Benbradagh, at C 752 123. It should not be confused with Legavannon Pot, which is about three miles further north on the Dungiven-Ringsend road. From Legananam Pot follow the road south-east for a few hundred yards, then turn right and follow a recently-made tarred road right up to the shoulder of Benbradagh. This road was made to serve the former American communications station on the top of Benbradagh, now made obsolete by satellites. The road carries little traffic and gives pleasant open views. At the crest of the hill it forks right, pointing towards the summit (the left fork turns down to Dungiven) and then it turns right again below the summit. At this point leave the road and follow the fence up to the summit (1,535 ft). After exploring the escarpment walk a little south of east from the summit to the top (south) end of Lenamore Forest; at the time of writing a green-painted square building, part of the abandoned communications station, gives a useful line of direction. From this south end of the forest there is a track through it. Follow the track right down to the north (about 1½ miles), until you come to the road again. Turn right and walk south-east until you come to Legananam Pot.

Distance: 7½ miles.   Ascent: 950 ft.   Walking Time: 3 hours.

37. NINE SUMMITS   The Sperrin Mountains form two broad ridges of hills, the higher being smothered in peat and the lower for the most part covered with coarse grass and heather. They are divided by the east-west line of the Glenelly valley. The northerly, higher ridge includes Dart and Sawel and is the subject of this walk. The Sperrins have a peculiar beauty that is hard to describe. It has something to do with the soft atmosphere, and the haunting light created by late sun after showers of rain. The dominant colours tend to be brown and purple, both associated with peat and heather and ploughed land.

I know no part of Ireland that has so many hills whose names begin with mullagh, a summit. The name seems to apply suitably to the Sperrins which are always rounded, never sharp and dramatic. This walk might be called the Nine Mullaghs, for all the nine hills covered are similar in form, though they rise to a modest crescendo in Sawel at 2,240 ft.

Start at Plumbridge. (If no accommodation is available, then you may stay at or near Newtownstewart.) A glance at the one-inch map will show that there are a dozen ways of getting on to the Mullaghs. I chose one of them so that you might see the stone circles, but it is not necessarily the best.

Walk up the Glenelly road for two miles and take the track that runs up the east side of the Glensass Burn; the track turns to the right and then goes due north up the mountain.

Three hundred yards on the left at H 522 925 and at a height of 750 ft are two concentric stone circles, with diameters of 30 and 60 ft, surrounding a small cairn 12 ft across. On excavation this revealed a small cist containing the cremated bones of a youth. A loose slab which may once have covered the cist bears a cup-mark. From the south side of the

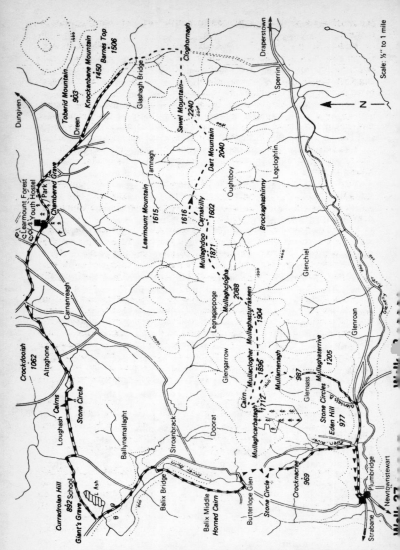

outer circle, which has small uprights set close together, an alignment of 15 uprights 3 ft high stretches for 75 ft. Immediately east is a small cairn. Another double circle lies 50 yards to the east, and 100 yards to

74

the north are two circles with conspicuously tall stones at the point of contact.

Follow the track to 987 ft and climb up the ridge of Mullaghmenagh. Curve round to the left above the 1,500 ft contour, generally north-west, to the top of Mullaghcarbatagh (1,712 ft). There is a cairn one-third of a mile away to the north-west. It is a typical circular hill-top cairn, four to five ft high and 36 ft across.

You now have the situation beloved by most hill walkers of having arrived on a peak (albeit a mullagh, not high even by Irish standards) and being able without any great ascent, descent or trouble, to climb eight more peaks. Very little direction is needed; just go roughly east.

From the cairn go south-east for a mile to Mullaghclogher (1,896 ft). Then, with more of a dip this time, another 1¼ miles to Mullaghasturrakeen (1,904 ft).

Next you climb north-east to Mullaghclogha (2,088 ft) and on to Mullaghdoo (1,871 ft). Here you turn east to Carnakilly (1,602 ft) which brings you to the Tyrone/Londonderry boundary on which you continue for the rest of the climb.

Climb north-north-east to 1,616 ft and drop down east crossing a track that connects two valleys and which you could take if the weather had turned bad. You now have the two highest Sperrin peaks to climb. Dart is now 600 ft above you, but it is a gradual climb east-south-east for a mile. On the top the peat is worn into hags and the going is usually wet.

From the top of Dart (2,040 ft) you go north-east to Sawel, a further 1¼ miles of boggy, worn peat. The name Sawel (*Sabhal*, a barn) suggests a barn church such as Patrick built at Saul, near Downpatrick.

Here you come to the only considerable drop in this northern range of the Sperrins. Below is the Glenelly valley going east to Draperstown and the comparatively flat and fertile lands of the Bann basin. To the south is the parallel lower range of the Sperrins, and to the north are the wooded glens of the foothills, leading on to the basalt escarpments of Benbradagh and Binevenagh.

Drop down east to the road, running from the hamlet of Sperrin south to north to the village of Park, which divides the range in two. You now have a five-mile walk downhill to Park and a further three-quarters of a mile to the Youth Hostel at Learmount.

Distance: 19½ miles. Ascent: 3,400 ft. Walking Time: 9 hours.

38. LEARMOUNT Y.H. TO PLUMBRIDGE: ARCHAEOLOGICAL SITES

After the exertions of Walk 37 a walk in search of archaeological sites in the northern foothills of the Sperrins may provide an interesting and pleasant diversion. It will include a number of small steep-sided glens. Looking for ancient monuments brings one in touch with local people. You may get on to other subjects, such as folklore and farming methods, old and new, and you will learn something from these encounters.

From the hostel at Learmount you may, as an option not to interfere with the main business of the day, wish first to look at what remains of the 'chambered grave' at Park marked on the one-inch map at C 590 020. The remains of a large wedge-shaped chamber grave were to be seen some years ago, but may now have been further disturbed.

Leave the hostel and walk west across Kilgort Bridge, continuing for just over 1¼ miles to Carnanbane. Take the road on the left and continue for 2½ miles. In a field on the left is one site; in a field on the right is another. The monument on the right at C 515 015, immediately north of the road, was excavated in 1938 and is described by Evans. The cairn is about 55 ft in diameter and is called Cashelbane, the White Fort. The south side is indented by a semi-circular forecourt, opening into a wedge-shaped gallery-grave 20 ft long. The cairn was apparently surrounded by a fosse with an internal diameter of 60 ft. Beaker sherds, arrow-heads and bowls were found. Evans placed the monument in the Early Bronze Age.

These wedge-graves are widespread in Ireland. They usually lack a court, but have straight sides and front and an antechamber, and tend to be shaped like a wedge in plan: hence their name. When they have been excavated the grave-goods place them at the end of the Neolithic period, when copper and bronze were coming into use.

To the north of this site there are the remains of other cairns. The whole area was formerly rich in remains, including cists, megalithic chambers, round cairns, standing stones and stone circles.

On the left of the road, 200 yards south-east of Cashelbane, is a stone circle with an alignment of stones at a tangent (C 517 012).

Continue west for a little over a mile. Turn right and after 300 yards turn left. After a mile you will come to another wedge-grave marked 'Giant's Grave' on the one-inch map at C 483 009, 150 yards south-west of Loughash school. Lough Ash itself lies on the other side of the road. The entrance to the wedge-grave faces west and is divided into two parts by an upright on which are twelve cupmarks. The gallery, 23 feet long, is segmented. Excavation in 1938 revealed cremated human bones and with them a fragment of a bronze blade and sherds of an urn. In another part of the main chamber were the scattered cremated remains of at least two persons together with charcoal and pieces of pottery, including beakers and coarse neolithic ware. It was thought that the monument was unlikely to be older than 1500 B.C.

After half a mile turn south down the road in the direction of Plumbridge. This is attractive country with mixed farming in valleys, grazing on hillsides, and deep, bushy glens. Walk south for just over 1½ miles and then take a road to the right, crossing the Inver Burn. After 1½ miles up this glen, in Balix Middle townland, you climb up to the 800 ft contour (300 yards in from the road) to see the remains of a horned cairn at H 483 964. This cairn was about 73 ft by 40 ft. The horn, V-shaped, started in front of portal-stones. The wedge-shaped chamber was about 15 ft long.

At the head of the glen the road crosses the Inver Burn again. Turn left, and after 300 yards turn right up the narrow Butterlope Glen. At H 493 947 is a stone circle revealed in the course of peat-cutting. It consists of about fifteen uprights and is 40 ft in diameter. Immediately to the east is a long recumbent stone and further east are several uprights.

About a quarter of a mile south-west of this stone circle is another group of monuments at H 488 945 on the Meenerrigal Rocks. Climb up to these and you will find a wedge-grave set in a round cairn, diameter 35 ft, and surrounded by a stone circle with a diameter of 60 ft. It was excavated in 1937, but the grave proved to be roofless and its contents were few. The straight facade of the outer walling is typically rounded at the back. The gallery, 12 ft long, is segmented. The stone circle has seventeen uprights, 3 ft high.

Return to the track and go south down the glen of the Eden River to the Glenelly valley and walk a mile west to Plumbridge.

Distance: 18 miles (excluding Park).   Ascent: 950 ft.   Walking Time: 7 hours.

39. THE GLENELLY VALLEY
I am calling this walk the Glenelly Valley because, for almost the whole of it, you will be within sight of this long valley. The first half of the walk is along slightly undulating hills which never rise much above 1,400 feet; the second is along a winding and unfrequented road at 600—700 feet; both overlook the valley and across it to Dart and Sawel and all the Mullaghs of earlier walks.

From the hamlet of Sperrin drive south across the river and take the left turn above Sperrin Lodge. The road climbs steeply and you should stop and park just after the first cattle-grid at H 643 938. Climb up the road to the highest point of the col (1,052 ft). Start climbing west from here up Corratary Hill; down on the left you will see the tiny Lough Lark. The going is soft and boggy, but the heather helps to stiffen it and there is the bright green bilberry plant (with dark purple fruit in August). Climb to the top (1,261 ft) and continue west-south-west along the boggy heathery top for a mile and a half to Quiggy Hill (1,256 ft). When you are up here you realise how extensive the Sperrins are, for you are surrounded by hills and they shade from green to grey to blue and to grey again.

Continue in the same direction for another mile and a half to Clogherny Top (1,338 ft). The ridge conveniently keeps at a high level and you continue along it south-west. (Your walk here moves from Sheet 2 to Sheet 5 in the one-inch O.S. series). It is a mile and a half from Clogherny Top to Mullaghbollig (1,456 ft), the highest point on the walk. Here you have views to the south over new country – the Owenkillew valley into which flows the Glenlark River, the Coneyglen Burn and the Carnanransy Burn. Beyond are range after range of low hills with, to the south-west, the bulky Mullaghcarn and the Forest of Gortin Glen.

Turn west and make your way down steeply to Barnes Gap, with its dark pines. When you come to the road turn north. There are no houses in sight as the road winds through the narrow gap, one of the loneliest places in the Sperrins.

Turn right and right again through the townland of Upper Barnes.

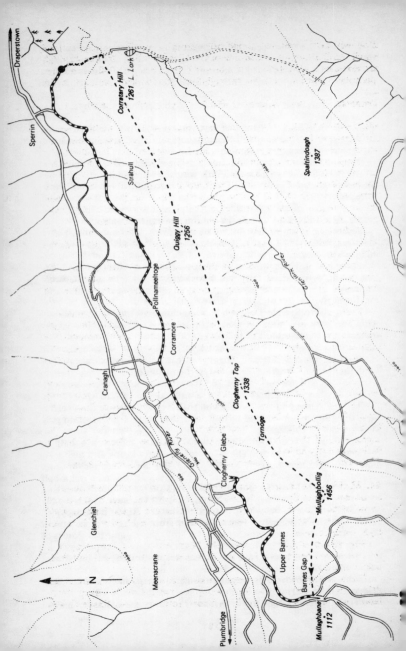

You will have seven and a half miles from Barnes Gap along the road which winds along the south side of the Glenelly valley. You go through the townlands of Clogherny Glebe and Corramore past Pollnameeltoge, the hole in the bare hillside, through Strahull townland and back to the car.

Distance: 15 miles. Ascent: 1,350 ft. Walking Time: 6 hours.

40. CARNANELLY
After the last, heavy walk (or perhaps as an alternative to it) this one will be comparatively easy. It will provide an experience of the upper, even more lonely, reach of the Glenelly valley.

From the hamlet of Sperrin drive south across the river and take the left turn above Sperrin Lodge. Park just after the first cattle-grid at about 800 feet at H 643 938. Climb up the road to about the highest point of the col (1,052 ft) and cross the fence on the left at a point where you can go along the edge of the plantation which, though well-grown, is additional to that shown on the one-inch O.S. map.

Underfoot is boggy, but less so as you climb. The trees absorb the moisture and if you find the going very wet you will find it drier at the edge of the forest.

Climb up past the planting to the top of Mullaghbane (the fair hill), just over 1,500 ft. From here you have a new view of the mountains to the north with the slopes sweeping away in a variety of subtle blue and green and grey.

Make south-east for the higher ground of the ridge of Carnanelly, with the little Altaloran Glen on your left. Having attained the ridge, make east along it to the top at 1,851 ft. To the east the view opens out right across the plains of the Lough Neagh and Lower Bann basin. All the way round southwards are more and more sweeps of the lower Sperrins. Slieve Gallion is prominent to the south-east.

Continue east along the ridge of Carnanelly for a mile. You are now on the Londonderry/Tyrone border and you keep on it as you climb over Slieveavaddy (1,605 ft). Go down (still on the county border) to Lough Ouske and, following a track for the later part of the way, drop to the Glenelly valley road. You now have a walk of 4½ miles down the upper part of the Glenelly valley to Sperrin. From there you have a little over half a mile up to your car.

Distance: 10½ miles. Ascent: 1,450 ft. Walking Time: 4½ hours.

41. SLIEVE GALLION
Slieve Gallion is a rather remote mountain, an outlier of the Sperrins. It lies tantalisingly to the west of the broad basin of the Lower Bann and is very prominent in the landscape of south Londonderry, east Tyrone and mid-Antrim. And yet it is not high, being at most 1,729 ft.

The towns nearby — Magherafelt, Moneymore and Draperstown — all owe something to the London Companies in their layout and their public buildings.

From Magherafelt or Moneymore drive to a cross-roads at Brackagh Bridge (H 839 894). Drive south along the road towards Tirgan townland. Then drive west up the Tirgan road towards Windy Castle (1,216

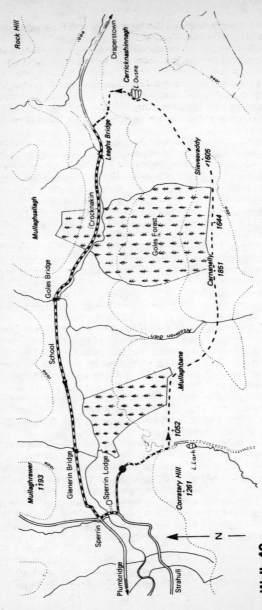

Walk 40

N

ft). The road continues round the base of the latter and winds up to about 1,450 ft. Park here at H 812 887.

You will now see what was not obvious from below, that there are two peaks, and you can decide which to climb first. I suggest the more northerly. It is an easy climb, the turf soft and springy. Apart from the more recent communications erection there are two disturbed cairns. One is described in the Preliminary Survey as 36 ft in diameter and 7 ft high with no sign of a chamber. This is at the summit (1,623 ft). The second is 200 yards south-west and was built on a small plateau. It had a chamber.

There is an extensive view from this north summit of Lough Neagh and the broad valley of the Lower Bann. Westwards are the Sperrins, sweeping away in wave upon wave of hills. Below are the towns of south Derry: Moneymore, Magherafelt, Desertmartin, Tobermore and Draperstown.

Turn south again down the hill and go along the turf-cutters' road towards the south peak. Here once more, as in the Second World War, with fuel scarce and expensive, the turf cutters are at work. They are cutting vertically with the 'lug' spade or horizontally with the 'breast' spade. The wet, cut turves are conveyed by barrow a few feet away to the high uncut bank and there spread to dry. Breasting is easier on the back and is quicker, since the turf can be kept on the spade and placed on the barrow. Nowadays a small tractor with a handy conveyance is sometimes used. The farmers have their own share of the blanket bog and in good weather they work all day, their families bringing a picnic at midday and tea-time.

Climb to the top where there is an Ordnance Survey trigonometrical pillar at 1,729 ft. From the summit there are fresh views of the south Sperrins, and you can see Lough Fea, the lovely little Carndaisy Glen, and Cookstown. Return down the turf-cutters' road to the car.
Distance: 3½ miles.   Ascent: 450 ft.   Walking Time: 1½ hours.

42. LOUGH NAVAR FROM CHURCH HILL   There are at least seven country houses with approved accommodation in the Church Hill/Blaney district which is an additional reason for planning a loop walk in this area.

Starting from the Church Hill Post Office (H 112 558), walk along the road which runs north-north-west for 1¾ miles. At the end of the road, at about 350 ft, you come to private land, but with permission you may go on through to the forest. In the forest you come to the line of the former county road. This line runs at 300 to 400 ft through the forest until it comes down to the shore road. A few fundred yards along this road you come to the Magho car park and there is a steep zig-zag way up the escarpment to the viewpoint at H 062 577.

The view from Magho cliffs is surprisingly extensive; it includes the islands of Lower Lough Erne, the Sperrins, Muckish, Errigal, the Blue Stacks, Donegal Bay and the Dartry Mountains. From the viewpoint follow the Ulster Way signs through the forest. The path goes west across moorland which is broken by a series of sandstone cliffs and

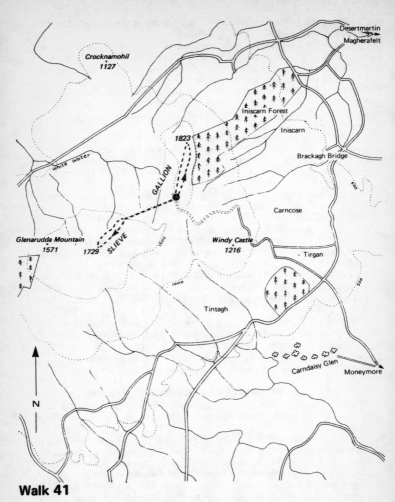

Desertmartin
Magherafelt

Crocknamohil
1127

White Water

Iniscarn Forest

Iniscarn

1823

Brackagh Bridge

GALLION

Carncose

SLIEVE

Glenarudda Mountain
1571

1729

Windy Castle
1216

Tirgan

Tintagh

Carndaisy Glen

Moneymore

N

Walk 41

young plantations of sitka spruce and lodgepole pine. It passes Meena-
meen Lough, Lough Navar and turf banks which are still being worked.
Meadow pipits are common and you should see curlew, stonechat,
grouse, and possibly a hen harrier. Greenland white-fronted geese visit
the lakes in winter. The route climbs to Melly's rock and leads to a
sweathouse, the Irish forerunner of the sauna. There is a chalybeate
spring well near the county road.

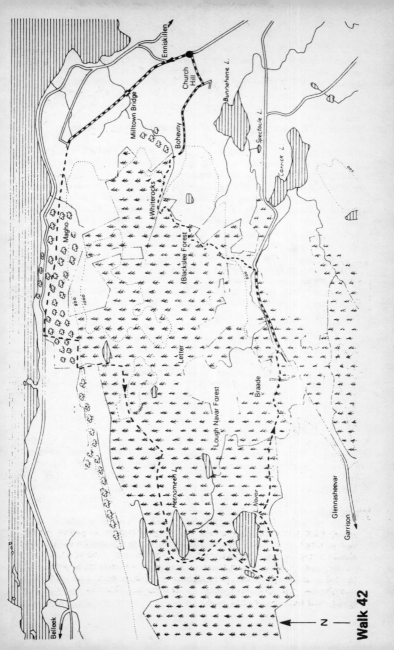

Walk 42

N

You leave the Ulster Way here and go left on the county road for almost a mile, when you come to the main car entrance to the forest park. Go in here and follow the road until there is a track on the right. Follow this track through the very pleasant Whiterocks area of the forest, and bear east till you come to the exit at Bohevny. On your right are Bunnahone Lough and the tiny Spectacle Lough, as you follow the road from here to Church Hill.

Distance: 16 miles.   Ascent: 900 ft.   Walking Time: 6 hours.

43. LARGALINNY, CARRICK LOUGH AND CORREL GLEN   If you have no transport, you can still do this walk from Church Hill where there is overnight accommodation. If you have a car, I suggest you park it at the entrance to Lough Navar Forest Park at H 074 547.

Walk westwards along the county road for nearly a mile and then join the Ulster Way by turning left into the forest. The Way follows first a forest road and then paths worn in the past by the driving of cattle from valley to valley. You pass Largalinny Lough and again join the forest road before entering a wood of old spruce.

Climb out of the valley over the old turf banks. Pass Lough Fadd on the left. In the forest there are sitka spruce, pine and Lawson's cypress, and there are also beech and the western hemlock (Tsuga). This conifer, introduced into Britain from the Pacific coast of North America in 1853, has a multitude of little pendent branches and a graceful pendent whip-like leader.

There are pheasants to be seen and heard as they rise heavily from the undergrowth and you may get the strong smell of a fox hanging in the air. You should see badger setts, but you will only see the badger if you wait quietly after dusk.

When your path comes to the Doagh road, leave the Ulster Way and walk along the road to your left. The road winds downhill towards Doagh Lough. There is a rich flora in these damp meadow lands, and there is a brightness in the landscape that you always get in limestone country. Down on the left is Monawilkin Lough, also of great interest to the botanist.

Leave the road south-east of that lough at about H 086 526 and follow a path that wanders north east across the hillocky country towards Carrick Lough. The lake is beautifully situated, with grassy limestone hills rising from one shore and heathery sandstones from the other. The limestones and sandstones yield a galaxy of plants. On the limestone hill above the lough is the Irish Eyebright and other lime-loving plants, and about the lough juniper is growing.

On the south shore of the lough are the ivy-covered remains of Aghamore Church. The church, which was built in the latter half of the fifteenth century, is very ruinous; only parts of the north and south walls remain.

Running up from the west end of the lake is Correl Glen, a deep cut in the sandstone. The ravine is choked with huge blocks of sandstone, covered by a canopy of ancient oak and birch-trees; boulders and tree-trunks are smothered in mosses and ferns. Hazel, holly, ash, and rowan

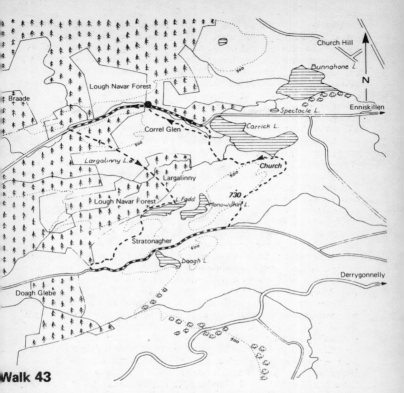

Walk 43

also flourish. You may either go in at this east end or go up the county road and enter by the usual entrance which is opposite where your car is parked. This is a National Nature Reserve; it covers fifty-eight acres, includes a nature trail and is well worthy of a separate full exploration. **Distance: 8 miles. Ascent: 1,050 ft. Walking Time: 3½ hours.**

44. BIG DOG AND KNOCKMORE Park your car at the little car park on the Doagh Road where there is an Ulster Way sign, and walk west along the road for 1½ miles to the point on your left where you go down to the entrance to the forest, and follow the forest road southwards. The boggy land on which the forest is planted has a number of lonely loughs; you pass two of these on your left, Lough Doo (the black lough) and Lough Nabrackboy (the lough of the yellow rising-ground). The track winds to the summits of Little Dog and Big Dog, small lumpy hills of just over 800 ft.

As you climb Little Dog you have on your right Meenagleragh

85

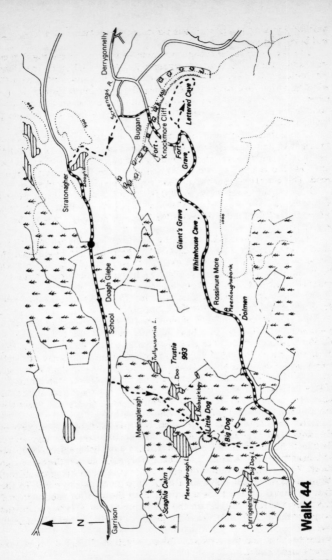

Lough. At a point half a mile to the west of this lough, at H 022 508, is the Scaghla Cairn, a long disturbed cairn, oval in shape, several feet high, 70 ft long and 45 ft wide. At Carrigeenbrack, one-third of a mile west of Big Dog Lough on your right, are the remains of a long cairn and burial chamber.

You leave the forest when you come to the road at the Big Dog car park and turn left towards Derrygonnelly. After 300 yards the Ulster Way enters the forest on your right. You pass this and continue on the winding, rising road through the townland of Rossinure More. You now begin to get views of Lower Lough Erne and its islands. There are a number of prehistoric remains to be seen if you take the trouble to look for them:

1. A dolmen a quarter of a mile east of Rossinuremore school on the right of your road. It has a large capstone supported on small stones.

2. A 'Giant's Grave' in Rossinurebeg, a quarter of a mile north-east of a limestone cave known as Whitehouse Cave, on the left of your road. This is a megalithic burial chamber, but is very incomplete.

3. A megalithic chamber at 600 ft, 1¼ miles south-west of Buggan Cross Roads, one-third of a mile west of the sharp turn in the road which skirts Knockmore (H 081 504). This was possibly a wedge-shaped grave.

4. At 900 ft immediately to the north of Knockmore summit — a cave with scribings. The mouth is 10 ft high by 5 ft broad, and the height gradually diminishes for over 20 ft to about 5 ft at the end. On both sides are scribings cut into the walls, but particularly on the left side. They include interlaced crosses and knots.

5. Two earthen ring forts, each about 90 yards to the west of your road as you walk round below Knockmore.

One of the main objects of your walk is to climb Knockmore, a prominent and lovely limestone hill. Go in from the public road at H 083 504 and climb the track that winds up to the face of the hill. Near the top is the lettered cave described above, and there are wide views of the lakes and islands and the long reaches of the Fermanagh plateaux. You will find clefts in the rock which make mini-habitats for plants such as the yew tree. There is mossy saxifrage and alpine enchanter's nightshade, the Irish eyebright and plenty of mountain avens, while blue moss grass is growing on the hill.

After you have explored Knockmore and perhaps one or two of the antiquities I have mentioned, you should take the way down (H 086 508) to Mr Acheson's farm, closing gates where necessary, and seek his permission to cross the plank-and-wire bridge over the Screenagh River. With his permission you may walk up through his grazing-land, taking care of fences, towards a long hill with an escarpment. To the right of this is Doagh Lough. Go round to the right of the lough and make for the lane marked on the 1" map which will take you to the Doagh road. Go left on the road for just over three-quarters of a mile to your car.

Distance: 10.8 miles.   Ascent: 750 ft.   Walking Time: 4 hours (excluding antiquities).

45. MARBLE ARCH, TILTINBANE AND CUILCAGH For most visitors to Fermanagh, if they motor west along the Clogher Valley

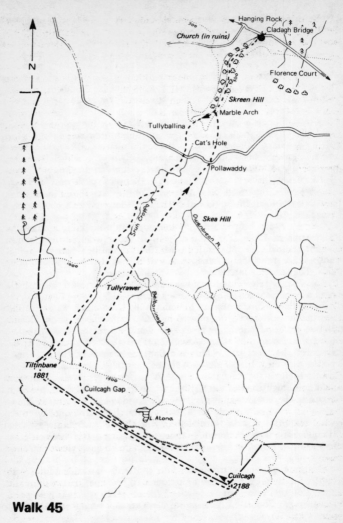

Walk 45

through Clogher and Fivemiletown, their first view of Fermanagh is the distant blue ridge of Cuilcagh (pronounced Kulk-yach). As you explore South and West Fermanagh this great ridge, which stretches for 2½ miles, dominates the landscape. It should be included in two walks, the whole ridge in this one, and the peak only in Walk 46.

For this walk and the next you should carry a compass, as much of the boggy, heathery terrain above 800 ft is without definition, the slopes are gradual and uncertain, and the rivers, which should be a guide, tend to disappear. In these conditions mist can blot out everything.

Park your car at the convenient parking place, at the foot of the Cladagh Glen, at Cladagh Bridge (H 128 357). Walk up this very lovely glen down which pours the Cladagh River. The woods of birch and ash are rich in sedges and helliborines. Half a mile up a torrent rushes in from the left. After another half mile you reach the Marble Arch, a lofty bridge of limestone under which pour the waters of the Sruh Croppa and other rivers.

On Cuilcagh there are many limestone caves into which the rivers disappear. The Millstone, which forms the summit of Cuilcagh, gives way to Yoredale rocks and this in turn to limestone. The streams which come down from Cuilcagh and Trien vanish underground as soon as they strike the soluble limestone. Their further courses are shown by occasional collapses of the cave-roofs, resulting in deep tree-filled depressions, called polls or swallow-holes, in the undulating ground. At the bottom of some of these you can see the streams coming from a cave on one side and re-entering the rock at the other. It seems that all the branches continue to make their exit at the Marble Arch and pour down the Cladagh Glen.

Above the Arch the river forms an underground lake, but a little further up large swallow-holes allow entrance into a complicated cave. This was first explored by a Frenchman, E. A. Martel, in 1897, and then, more thoroughly, in 1907–8 by R. L. Praeger and others. Cavers' clubs explore the vast chambers, with their stalactites and stalagmites, and the underground lakes. Care should be taken of caves and holes, particularly by lone walkers and by school parties.

Climb out of the woods above the Marble Arch in a south-west direction, and continue on the track for a quarter of a mile, then turn south and go to the Cat's Hole into which the principal river, the Sruh Croppa, pours and disappears. This will be the first of many swallow-holes you will find on this and the next two walks. They are all interesting, for they provide a mini-habitat for a variety of plants, a haven from the bleak and often sodden mountain. Shortly after this you cross the Marlbank Loop, which provides motorists with good views of South Fermanagh.

Continue to climb south-south-west along the west side of the Sruh Croppa for three miles in the direction of Tiltinbane, the western end of the Cuilcagh ridge. The going over the heathery slopes is heavy and frequently very wet but, when you climb steeply to the top at Tiltinbane (1,881 ft), you are rewarded by a very fine view. Here you are on the border of Fermanagh and Cavan, and of Northern Ireland and the Republic, and you continue on it as you walk south-east for 2½ miles along the ridge of Cuilcagh. There is a steep escarpment most of the way to the top at 2,188 ft. On the south side there is a cliff at the Tiltinbane end and again at the east end. All along the ridge you have to the east and north a magnificent panorama of the whole of Fermanagh and beyond, the islands of Upper Lough Erne, and the dim reaches of Lough Oughter, the beginning of the Erne system. The lonely Lough Atona lies below the cliff. To the south you have new vistas of hills and plains, Lough Allen and the Shannon. The source of the Shannon is 2½ miles north-west of Tiltinbane.

One way of returning would be to go back the way you came, but the way I suggest on the sketch map is to return along the ridge for three-quarters of its length to the Cuilcagh Gap which gives the first break in the northern escarpment and go down from there to Tully-rawer in a direction roughly parallel to that of your ascent. You cross the Belbarrinagh River and again you will see a number of swallow-holes. Finally you come to Pollawaddy, the dog's hole. Cross the Marlbank Loop and make for the woods and the path to the Marble Arch. Continue down the Cladagh Glen to your car.

Distance: 14 miles.   Ascent: 1,950 ft.   Walking Time: 7 hours.

46. CUILCAGH FROM FLORENCE COURT

This walk has three facets. First, it gives a frontal view of one of the finest classical houses in Ulster. Second, it enables you to walk through 200-year-old decid-uous woodland of great beauty, a habitat for a rich woodland flora and insect life. Third, it introduces you to this great hulk of a mountain, Cuilcagh. It is a heavy walk, a fact for which I have allowed in giving a more generous allocation of walking time (in this and the preceding walk) than would be allotted by the usual bare rule of thumb.

Leave your car in the car park which, at the time of writing, is being prepared as part of the Florence Court Forest Park (H 178 348). The Forest Service is planning a walk to Cuilcagh and it should be signposted by the time this book is published. If so, it will help you in following the walk that I describe here. Walk No. 45 is one way of climbing Cuilcagh; this is another.

If you have not already visited Florence Court House and its gardens, which belong to the National Trust, you must do so, but preferably on another day, as there is so much to see. (The house and gardens are open from April to September, every day except Friday, 2–6 p.m.)

The forest walk will take you round the front of the house and close to the recently constructed ha-ha, an 18th century device for protect-ing the view of those in the house from being spoiled by fencing. The house was completed by John Cole, Baron Mount Florence, grandfather of the first Earl of Enniskillen, in 1764 and is strictly classical in style, consisting of a compact centre block of three storeys joined by straight corridors of seven arched openings to two flanking pavilions. These, of one-storey height, have pedimented fronts and pitched lead roofs. The interior has beautiful rococo plasterwork restored by the National Trust after a fire in 1955.

Your way winds round the gardens of the house and along the little Larganess River before bearing right to Kerrshill Wood. Here in a clear-ing is the original Florence Court Yew, the progenitor of the trees *(taxus baccata fastigiata)* now found all over the world. It is one of a pair

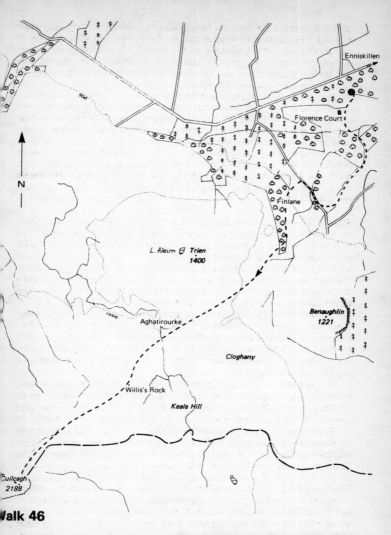

Enniskillen

Florence Court

Finlane

L. Aleim & Trien
1400

Benaughlin
1221

Aghatirourke

Cloghany

Willis's Rock

Keala Hill

Cuilcagh
2188

Walk 46

found by a kinsman of my own, George Willis, a tenant of Lord Mount
Florence who was living above and behind Florence Court House on the
high land of Aghatirourke. It is a freak in that it can only be propagated
by cuttings, the seedlings reverting to the common female berry-bearing
type. He found the two on a cleft limestone rock on the mountain. The

91

one he planted in his own garden died after a hundred years; the other is this one. In Kerrshill Wood there is an old Oriental plane and there are turkey oak, Wellingtonia and field maple.

You go south along the Finglass River through the edge of the Cottage Wood. Here are many fine old oak and some silver fir. The walk continues along the river through a great variety of willows, birch, ash and laurel. Go west for a while and then round north-west along an old country road and into Glen Wood with many fine mature oaks. You now turn left and go uphill into Finlane and the Cove Wood which has larch and spruce and old beech. Above Cove Wood there is rowan and hazel scrub under the escarpment.

Going gradually uphill you climb on to the moors. Continue south-west along the lower slopes of Trien, a broad, boggy mountain. The going is heavy through Aghatirourke, over heathery, mossy and often wet ground, but it is broken up by an occasional *poll* or swallow-hole where the limestone roof of an underground river has fallen in and the hole is growing rowan-trees, foxgloves and ferns. About the 1,250 ft contour there are some outcrops of limestone rocks. One of these, with a narrow and deep cleft, is known as *carraig na madadh*, the rock of the dog, or Willis's Rock. It was here in this cleft that George Willis found the Florence Court Yew (about H 143 297).

You have still over 1½ miles to go to the top, and near the summit it is very steep. There is a steep cliff on the south and east sides. On the top is an Ordnance Survey pillar and you are here on the border with Cavan and the Republic. I have described the view in Walk No. 45.

I suggest that you return by the same route, but if the day is fine you may go over Trien just to get some extra height on your way back. Trien is 1,400 ft and there is a small lough, Aleim, on the top.

Your day on Cuilcagh should be enlivened by the sight of an occasional grouse, by the pruck of the raven and perhaps by the sight of a peregrine. You should also see the meadow pipit and the wheatear. On the wet rocks you will find the delicate rosettes of the starry saxifrage, and on the heath in the autumn you will find the edible red berries of cowberry. There is plenty of sphagnum moss and you will find club-moss with its upright spikes of spore-cases. On your way back you should explore some of the swallow-holes. Return by the path below Finlane and around Florence Court House to the car park.

Distance: 12½ miles (excluding Trien).   Ascent: 2,000 ft.   Walking Time: 6½ hours.

47. BENAUGHLIN

Benaughlin is only 1,221 ft high, but because of its commanding shape, its comparative aloofness, its outstanding views and its heather cover it is a mountain which should be climbed.

It could be climbed from Florence Court, but the best way is perhaps from Gortalughany. Take your car to H 196 301 on the Enniskillen-Swanlinbar road, and turn west up the broad and later twisting road, parking at the viewpoint at Gortalughany, about 1,100 ft, at H 165 300. Walk on north-west by the turf-cutters' road for half a mile. Leave this track and go north-east across the moors for about half a

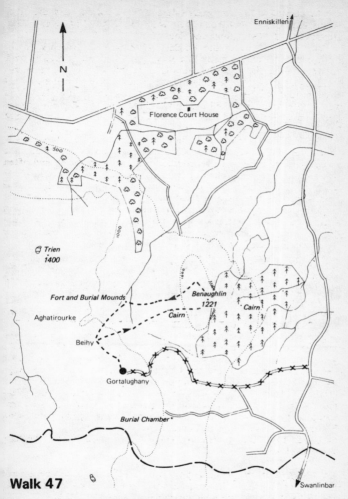

N↑

Florence Court House

⚑ Trien
·1400

Fort and Burial Mounds

Aghatirourke

Beihy

Benaughlin
1221

Cairn

Cairn

Gortalughany

Burial Chamber

Walk 47

↘Swanlinbar

mile in the general direction of Benaughlin. The ground begins to fall and you should go down to the north of the wooded slope above some cultivated land. Farming here is difficult, so take particular care of fencing and gates. Mr James Burleigh is the owner of the whole of the Beihy townland over which you are walking and his farmhouse and outbuildings are below you on your right. Go down the hill and with his permission you should cross to the north of his farmyard and make for the neat circular wall for enclosing cattle. From here it is a simple climb to the cairn marked on the 1" map at 900 ft. It is 10 ft high with a diameter of 50 ft. When excavated in 1883 it was found that a shallow fosse surrounded it and that it contained a large central cist (6 ft by 4 ft). A number of small cists were found, all with cremations. Sherds of food vessels pointed to an early to middle Bronze Age date.

The hill is covered with heather and the climbing is much firmer than on Cuilcagh and Trien, and on arrival at the top there is a fine view of the woods below, the small green fields of South Fermanagh, and the wooded islands of Upper Lough Erne. On the top is an Ordnance Survey pillar, and nearby is lying the gravestone of a servant of 'Lord E. Stuart'.

There is a steep cliff on the east side and you should explore the upper slopes of this before returning over the top and going down due west into the little valley. Climb up west to nearly 800 ft and in some rocky ground at about H 167 312 there is a ring-fort and a number of mounds known as 'Giant's Graves'. Like so many other prehistoric sites in Co. Fermanagh, both of these were recorded by Lady Dorothy Lowry-Corry of Castle Coole. The first she described as an earth and stone fort or cashel, the longest diameter being 33 yards. The second she thought covered the remains of burial cairns. These remote recumbent tombs in Aghatirourke townland have not yet been excavated.

As you climb back across Beihy in a generally south-west direction to about 1,100 ft you will come across an occasional swallow-hole which you will notice by the sudden emergence of small trees such as rowan. Return by the turf-road to your car.

Distance: 4½ miles.   Ascent: 800 ft.   Walking Time: 2½ hours.

Bibliography

Belfast and County Down Railway Co., *Guide to County Down and the Mourne Mountains,* Belfast, 1920.

Chart, D. A., Evans, Estyn, and Lawlor, H. C., *A Preliminary Survey of the Ancient Monuments of Northern Ireland,* Belfast, 1940.

Evans, Estyn, *Prehistoric and Early Christian Ireland,* London, 1966.

Fitter, Richard and Alastair, and Blamey, Margerie, *Wild Flowers of Britain and Northern Europe,* London, 1974.

National Trust, *Guides to Cushendun and Giant's Causeway,* Belfast.

Peterson, Roger, Mountfort, Guy, and Hollom, P. A. D., *A Field Guide to the Birds of Britain and Europe,* London, 1954.

Praeger, R. L., *The Botanist in Ireland,* Dublin, 1934.

Praeger, R. L., *The Way that I Went,* Dublin and London, 1939.

Tempest, H. G., *Guide to Dundalk and District,* Dundalk, 1920.

The Automobile Association, *Touring Guide to Ireland,* London, 1976.

Ulster Architectural Heritage Society, *Glens of Antrim,* Belfast, 1971.

Ulster Architectural Heritage Society, *North Antrim,* Belfast, 1972.

Glossary of the more common Irish words used in Place Names

Abha, abhain (ow, owen)	river
Achadh (agha, augh)	field
Aill or *faill*	cliff
Alt	height or side of glen
Ard	height, promontory
Baile (bally)	town, townland
Bán (bawn, baun)	white
Barr	top
Beag (beg)	small
Bealach (ballagh)	pass
Beann (ben)	peak or pointed mountain
Bearna (barna)	gap
Beith (beith)	birch tree
Bignian	little peak
Bóthar (boher)	road
Bóthairín (borheen)	small, (unsurfaced) road
Breac (brack)	speckled
Brí (bree, bray)	hill
Buaile (booley)	summer dairy pasture
Bun	foot of anything, river mouth
Buí	yellow
Carn	pile of stones
Carraig (carrick)	a rock
Ceann (ken)	head, headland
Ceathramhadh (carrow)	quarter of land
Ceapach	plot of tillage ground
Cill	cell, church
Clár	plain, board
Cloch	stone
Clochóg	stepping stones
Cluain (cloon, clon)	meadow
Cnoc (knock, crock)	hill
Coill (kyle, kill)	wood
Coire	cauldron, corrie
Cor	rounded hill
Corrán (carraun)	sickel, serrated mountain
Cruach, cruachán	steep hill (rick)
Cúm (coum)	hollow, corrie
Dearg	red
Doire (derry)	oakgrove
Druim	ridge
Dubh (duff, doo)	black
Dún	fort, castle
Eas (ass)	waterfall
Eisc (esk)	steep, rocky gully
Fionn (fin)	white, clear
Fraoch (freagh)	heath, heather
Gaoith (gwee)	wind

Glas	green
Glais	streamlet
Gleann (glen)	valley
Gort	tilled field
Inbhear (inver)	river mouth
Inis	island
Lágh (law)	hill
Leac	flagstone
Leaca, leacán (lackan)	side of a hill
Leacht	huge heap of stones
Learg	side of a hill
Leitir (letter)	wet hillside
Loch (lough)	lake or sea inlet
Lug, lag	hollow
Machaire (maghera)	plain
Mael, maol (mweel)	bald, bare hill
Maigh	plain
Mám, madhm (maum)	pass
Más	long, low hill
Mór (more)	big
Muing	long-grassed expanse
Mullach	summit
Poll	hole, pond
Riabhach	grey
Rinn	headland
Rua, ruadh	red
Scairbh (scarriff)	shallow ford
Scealp	rocky cleft
Sceilig (skellig)	rock
Sceir (sker, *pl.* skerry)	rock, reef (Norse)
Sescenn (seskin)	marsh
Sean	old
Sliabh (slieve)	mountain
Spinc	pointed pinnacle
Srón	nose, noselike mountain feature
Sruth, sruthair, sruthán	stream
Stuaic (stook)	pointed pinnacle
Suí, suidhe (see)	seat
Taobh, taebh (tave)	side, hillside
Tír (teer)	land, territory
Teach	house
Tobar	well
Tor	tower-like rock
Torc	wild boar
Tulach	little hill